Mastering the Mind, Realising the Self

The spiritual guide
to true happiness and inner peace

Mastering the Mind, Realising the Self

The spiritual guide
to true happiness and inner peace

Stephen Sturgess

BOOKS

Winchester, UK
Washington, USA

First published by O-Books, 2017
O-Books is an imprint of John Hunt Publishing Ltd., Laurel House, Station Approach,
Alresford, Hants, SO24 9JH, UK
office1@jhpbooks.net
www.johnhuntpublishing.com

For distributor details and how to order please visit the 'Ordering' section on our website.

ISBN: 978 1 78535 526 4
978 1 78535 527 1 (ebook)
Library of Congress Control Number: 2016943151

A CIP catalogue record for this book is available from the British Library.

Design: Lee Nash

Printed and bound by CPI Group (UK) Ltd, Croydon, CR0 4YY, UK

CONTENTS

I dedicate this book with love and gratitude to my beloved spiritual guru Paramhansa Yogananda (1893–1952), the embodiment of grace, wisdom and love, who appeared to me in a superconscious dream in 1982, and his direct disciple Swami Kriyananda (1926–2013) who wisely taught and guided me for 30 years on the Kriya Yoga path of meditation.

The wholehearted practice of meditation brings deep bliss. This ever-new bliss is not born of desire; it manifests itself by the magic command of your inner, intuitive-born calmness. Manifest this serenity always.

Paramhansa Yogananda

Preface

Our souls long for infinite joy, infinite love and eternal peace, but under the illusion of *maya*, and false identification, we continually try to find that in the finite. We are unable to find it in the finite and so we feel frustrated, unfulfilled, and incomplete. Through not knowing and understanding our mind and the essential spiritual nature of who we are, we remain in restlessness, bondage and suffering. We seek this sense of completeness and happiness outwardly and objectively in the world through relationships, possessions, and in new adventures and experiences, but because they are all subject to change and are not lasting, we come away disappointed, not understanding the exact source of happiness. The true source of what we are seeking can only be found deep within us, and we can never feel truly happy, fulfilled and complete until we have discovered and realised our Divine nature. Spiritual realisation means first knowing who you are. Knowing and realising the higher truth of who you are is knowing God. This is our first priority in life.

Know your true purpose in life. Be happy with what you have, aspire to obtain what you need, and use everything to attain the highest purpose of life. Self-discovery and self-mastery (of the mind) begins with the mastery over your own mind. Understand your mind and its relationship to yourself and the world. Blessed with the power of will and determination, you are the creator of your own destiny. It is your own self-effort and aspiration for Truth that must be cultivated. Once you have that sincere desire and aspiration for Truth, divine grace will come to you and guide you on the spiritual path to inner freedom, Self- and God-realisation.

The mind is vital and important to us: it is connected to the senses and the instruments of the body; without it we would not be able to function in this world. The mind uses different mental functions: thinking, reasoning, observation, feeling, willing, remembering, and speculating. Your happiness and unhappiness, success and failure, knowledge and ignorance, strength and weakness all depend on the nature of your mind. The mind is the instrument of perception, anything you know you know through the mind.

There are some people who live in the world without the sight of their eyes, and others without being able to hear, or speak, or their legs are paralysed, unable to walk, but as long as they have use of their mind, they are still able function in the world.

The mind also plays an important role in your spiritual development. The development of the mind is important, because life's development means the development of the mind. Just as your body needs nourishing with natural wholesome food and regular exercise to stay healthy, so does your mind need to be regularly nourished, strengthened and enriched. Both the body and the mind need to be disciplined, trained and developed if they are going to be fit instruments for the spiritual Self, the Consciousness that is expressed through them, that is distinct from the psychophysical system of the mind, body and the senses.

Your mind is both the source of freedom and bondage. The wise use the mind as an instrument to attain freedom from bondage, but the ignorant, not knowing how to wisely train and develop the mind, become caught in bondage, bound to its likes and dislikes, its habits, and its uncontrolled desires. The body, mind and the senses need to be in a harmonious state. First the body needs to be disciplined and trained in healthy habits, then the senses, mind and ego should also be trained to serve the spiritual Self.

The mind is *not* self-luminous, and by nature it is *not* conscious-self-awareness. The mind *is not* the Self because it can be observed by the unchanging Self, the very basis for cognition. Both the body and the mind are of a material nature, but the mind is of a very fine and *subtle* nature and is formless and invisible; it is associated with the subtle body not the physical body. The mind is an inner instrument that reflects the light of Consciousness, of the Self. The power that lies at the core of the mind, that breathes life into it, and illuminates it, is the inner Knower, the Self or Consciousness. The mind is limited; the Self is unlimited. Most of the time the mind turns outward and takes on the form of the worldly objects, but in meditation, when the outward-flowing mind is turned inward, it merges in its Source and reflects the pure inner Consciousness.

This principle of eternal Consciousness (the Self) within you is immortal and is the self-existent Reality which is the basis of your consciousness of ego. The unchanging Self is the Witness to the three states of consciousness – waking, dreaming, and deep sleep – and is distinct from the ego-mind, body and senses. That Reality, the spiritual Self, is self-aware, and sees everything by its own light. This light of Consciousness is transmitted through your mind and through your senses to reveal all things to you. It gives intelligence to your mind and intellect. It gives the mind the power to think, listen, and understand.

The cause of suffering is forgetting to maintain a constant awareness of that highest Truth, the centre of Consciousness, the Self (*Ātmān*), the truth of our real nature. In separation from our Source of infinite Reality we experience sorrow and suffering; joined in unity we experience equanimity, contentment, peace and joy. You suffer because you are constantly identifying with your body, the objects of your mind, and the ego-personality. You suffer because you do not know your true nature – the unchanging immortal Self – which transcends the body-mind-ego.

Every person is an immortal spiritual being expressing their life through a material body, mind and senses. We are in this world to learn effectively, and to eventually awaken to complete awareness and knowledge of our true spiritual nature and ultimate Reality.

Spiritual life begins when you accept the necessity to aspire to know and realise directly the highest Truth. Your sincere and earnest desire to want to know Truth will keep you open to the inflow of the nature of truth in your own Self. If you have been leading an outward sensory life for a long time, do not expect to enter into this Truth immediately. It will take time, patience, perseverance, and a steady constant disciplined effort. There are obstacles to overcome, and conditions to remove, for a mind conditioned by a lifetime of a mistaken sense of self-identity, habits, behaviours, impulses, desires, wrong attitudes, and negative thinking is not easily transformed into an enlightened mind. At times it may not be easy to stay inspired, self-motivated, and self-disciplined to adhere to regimens of right living, healthy living, and spiritual practice (*sādhanā*) such as meditation. But when there is the intention and willingness to learn and to awaken to Self-realisation, progress can be steady and fast.

Meditation is very important. It gives immense joy! The joy or bliss (*ānanda*) you experience in meditation is greater than any worldly happiness. Just as a flame does not flicker where there is no wind, a mind that has become absorbed in the Self always remains blissful in the Self. The inner Self is God within us. The kingdom of God is the Divinity within you.

When your body sits comfortable and steady and settles into stillness, your breath and your mind become calm, and your mind becomes one-pointed and inward. In meditation you remain in the freedom of the present moment, abiding in your true spiritual nature of the Self, which is ever-existent, ever-conscious, ever-new Bliss (*Sat-Cit-Ānanda*). It is this joy or bliss experienced in meditation that every human being seeks, because the very nature of the Self *is* bliss (*ānanda*), and until we realise the true nature of our Self we will cling to our limited individuality and remain unenlightened.

On your spiritual path to inner freedom and Self- and God-realisation, this book will be a useful guide and source of inspiration toward understanding your mind and knowing your true nature. Read it not just once but many times to remind yourself of who you are and what your true purpose is. For it is only by constant remembrance of the divinity within you that you can live in that higher conscious awareness of your God-Self. Practise the *Raja Yoga* and *Kriya Yoga* techniques of prāṇāyāma, mantra and meditation to remove the mental and emotional obstacles from your mind – the thoughts, feelings, perceptions and objects – so that your inner light can shine to direct your attention to the Truth.

For a comprehensive study of the Yoga philosophy and techniques please read my book, *The Supreme Art and Science of Raja and Kriya Yoga.* For a primer to *Kriya Yoga*, read my book, *Yoga Meditation*; this has the techniques for preparing for *Kriya* Initiation.

This book is divided into five parts:

Part One: The Mind

The importance of the mind and training it is covered in this first part. The meaning of what is happiness, and what is the mind are discussed. The mind has four main functions (*manas*, *buddhi*, *ahaṁkāra*, and *citta*); these are explained as according to Yoga and Vedanta philosophy.

The five conditions of the mind and the nine distractions of the mind are also explained, and with the means to remove the obstacles to transform the mind. The ancient sage Patañjali has listed these in his *Yoga Sūtras*. Part One also covers desires and attachment: why do desires arise in us? And where do they arise from?

Habits are discussed, and how to overcome them and changing negative thoughts into positive thoughts.

Patañjali's Yoga Sūtras teachings on understanding *citta* (mind), *vṛttis* (mental modifications), *vāsanās* (subtle desires) or *saṁskāras* (subtle karmic impressions), and *kleśas* (afflictions) that produce the *vṛttis* are also covered in Part One.

Part Two: The Different States of Consciousness

The subject of change, death, and the different states of consciousness – waking (*jagrat*), dream (*svapna*), and dreamless deep sleep (*sushupti*) are the main topics discussed in Part Two.

Part Three: The Self

What is consciousness? Without consciousness there is no world to witness or experience. Part Three is about *you*, the inner infinite Self, that conscious awareness that is independent of the mind and its activities. The hindrances to realising your true nature of the Self are discussed.

Part Four: Meditation, the Path to Inner Peace and Bliss

Part Four discusses the purpose of life and gives the three main purposes toward finding true inner and outer fulfilment in life. It then explains why meditation is important and gives the necessary guidelines and techniques for inner transformation, such as the power of affirmation and how to pray effectively.

The practical guidelines like when, where, and how to sit for meditation are covered as well as the meditation techniques. A supreme concentration technique of *Kriya Yoga* is explained. This is followed by a guided deep meditation.

Part Five: Yoga Practices for Meditation

In the last part of this book certain effective Yoga techniques are given. These are the *Prāṇāyāma* techniques: Yoga breathing techniques to regulate, lengthen and expand the breath, and to harmonise the subtle life force within the body. The *Prāṇāyāma* techniques include: *Ujjayi prāṇāyāma* (victorious breath), and *Nāḍī śodhana* or *Anuloma Viloma prāṇāyāma* (alternate nostril breathing).

May this book inspire you in your search for that eternal Truth that is your Divine Source. May it give meaning and purpose to your life to aspire you to that highest Truth. May you have the inner strength and faith to patiently persevere until you are Self-realised. The supreme purpose of meditation is to attain the highest goal of life, the direct perception of the Supreme Self, the light of God-consciousness which removes ignorance and darkness arising from egoism. Meditate daily and remain in constant Self-awareness of your true nature; this is the direct way, beyond the mind and ego, to spiritual enlightenment.

With blessings, peace, happiness and joy to you!

Stephen Sturgess
London (UK)
February 2016

Part One

The Mind

'Man shall not live on bread alone'

A healthy mind and body are important, but physical nourishment and nurturing alone are not sufficient to give true and lasting happiness and joy and inner fulfilment; we also have spiritual needs. This is reflected in what Jesus said in the Bible, *"It is written: 'Man shall not live on bread alone, but on every word that proceedeth from the mouth of God'"* (Luke 4:4). Here Jesus was referring back to words that had already been said previously in the Old Testament of the Bible in Deuteronomy 8:3.

Real Happiness

> *True happiness is never to be found outside the Self. Those who seek it there are as if chasing rainbows among the clouds!*
> Paramhansa Yogananda, *How to Be Happy All the Time: The Wisdom of Yogananda, Volume 1*, Crystal Clarity Publishers, Nevada City, California, 2006

Real happiness is a direct knowledge of the nature of the Self. But everyone except those who are Self-realised are searching for it outside of themselves not knowing that it is an inner state of *being*. In fact, the natural state of the inner Self, your real identity and essential nature, is happiness, joy, peace, calmness and love. It is these divine qualities along with Light, Sound, Power and Wisdom, that we attribute to God, and by absorbing your consciousness in any of these primary qualities you can become attuned to the blissful God-Self within you that is *Sat-Cit-Ānanda* (ever-existing, ever-conscious, ever-new Bliss).

In the New Testament of the Bible it is said:

> *Do not conform any longer to the pattern of this world, but be transformed by the renewing of your mind. Then you will be able to test and approve what God's Will is – His good, pleasing and perfect Will.* Romans 12:2

How is the mind renewed? The mind is renewed through prayer, meditation, by practising spiritual practices (*sādhanā*) to remove the mental and emotional obstacles of the mind, and by cultivating an awareness of the presence of God in every moment in your life. This is how we spiritualise the mind. Then the mind becomes spiritually purified and renewed, freed from its bad habits, negative thoughts, its limitations, and conditioning. If your mind is not spiritually illumined you are kept in the darkness of ignorance, and are unable to achieve the true heart's desire of divine purpose and spiritual fulfilment.

If you can truly understand and have mastery over your finite mind, you will be able to go beyond it. Through daily deep meditation you will be able to transfer your consciousness from the finite to the infinite. That supreme eternal joy or Bliss (*Ānanda*) that we are all seeking is revealed only in the quietness of the mind and the stillness of the inner Self; it is there that you will find absolute Truth and everlasting joy. When you spiritually awaken to this reality you will know that it is futile to continue searching for happiness in anything outside, whether it be in a person, an object, or anything of this world – money, fame, power. Why? Because everything material of this world is transient; it is subject to change, and has a beginning and an end. It cannot promise you everlasting happiness and fulfilment. It is only when you concentrate on the true values of life that you will find true happiness. The more you are carried away by material desires and attachments to the pleasures of the world, the further you drift away from your spiritual centre, the divine inner Self. You will never be satisfied, fulfilled or content with only transitory satisfactions; in the end they will bring the seeds of disappointment, anxiety, worry, and sorrow ending in suffering. Desires can never be really fulfilled; they are only temporarily fulfilled. As soon as one desire has been temporarily satisfied, it is not long before the mind becomes restless again clamouring for satisfaction. It is a vicious cycle; restlessness creates desires, which creates further restlessness.

These desires create deep active impressions (*saṁskāras*) in the subconscious mind. They are like seeds sown into the ground, and at the right time they sprout and appear above the ground as a plant. These desire seed impressions or *saṁskāras* lie dormant deep in the mind; then, when the time or condition is right they appear in the conscious mind as full-blown desires, creating a powerful urge within us to have them fulfilled and satisfied. If the desire is not satisfied then, one becomes frustrated and even angry.

What is Happiness?

> *Happiness depends to some extent upon external conditions, but chiefly upon conditions of the inner mind. In order to be happy, one needs good health, an efficient mind, a prosperous life, the right work and, above all, an all-accomplishing wisdom. One cannot be happy just by holding the inner calm while completely ignoring the struggle for existence and the effort for success.*
> Paramhansa Yogananda, *How to Be Happy All the Time: The Wisdom of Yogananda, Volume 1*, Crystal Clarity Publishers, Nevada City, CA, 2006

You can never make happiness the object of your desire or pleasure. Happiness cannot be objectified; it cannot be separated from you as your object. Happiness is beyond mental pleasure; happiness transcends the mind and expresses itself in pleasure. When you desire an object thinking that it will give you happiness, it is only when the desired object has been gained that your mind comes to rest – your body, mind and senses become relaxed, and there is no longer a desire. There is then a sense of happiness, the real nature of happiness shines by itself.

That happiness you experience is actually the real nature of yourself, but you are not able to see it. The enjoyment of happiness is being one with it. Unbroken happiness is peace. The desire which impels you to search comes from that happiness itself – *'I am*

Happiness' is the nature of the innermost Self. To go beyond the object of pleasure which you think is the source of happiness, trace the source of happiness you have enjoyed, to your real nature, and know it to be an expression of your own eternal Self.

Your essential real nature is freedom, peace and happiness itself. When you are truly happy you feel connected, happy and complete in yourself, but as soon as this happiness becomes interrupted you again feel separated, dissatisfied. You feel that there is something missing from your life. And every time you try to fulfil your desires and satisfy your needs, and become busy avoiding everything that you dislike and find disagreeable to you, your mind becomes agitated and unhappy. Those who have found inner peace, contentment and joy, who are not dependent on the world to provide their happiness and joy, are truly free. Those who are slavishly dependent on their happiness and joy from the world outside of themselves are like a rudderless boat without a captain or a compass to guide it out of the storm. It is only those who have learned to identify themselves with the unchanging Reality behind the waves and storms of changing objects and events in life that rise above them to enjoy lasting happiness and joy. It is those who have gained mastery over their minds that successfully attain inner peace and joy no matter what changes happen around them.

When we are unhappy and dissatisfied it is because we are overly identified and preoccupied with our body, our ego-personality, our desires and sense-attachments. All our energy goes into our efforts in creating, finding and sustaining enjoyment, sense-gratification and pleasure. This preoccupation of outwardly seeking happiness and satisfaction through transitory and fleeting pleasures in the world can never be totally satisfying or totally fulfilling. Yet, time and time again we endlessly pursue in the belief that happiness, the joy that we experience, lies outside of us in the objects, things and persons of the world. We erroneously think that they are the source of our happiness.

> *Your soul, being the reflection of the ever-joyous Spirit, is happiness itself.*
> Paramhansa Yogananda, *How to Be Happy All the Time: The Wisdom of Yogananda, Volume 1*, Crystal Clarity Publishers, Nevada City, CA, 2006

Happiness can be no other than a state of mind, and states of mind are continually changing from one moment to the next. When the mind is agitated or restless, we feel anxious, a feeling of sorrow and unhappiness comes over us like a dark cloud blocking the light of joy. Conversely, when we feel calm, peaceful and content, we feel inner joy like the sun shining its light upon us. There is a difference between pleasure and happiness. Pleasure is something that the mind experiences. Happiness transcends the mind; it is your own real nature, the Self, of inner peace that you experience as happiness. In relation to the mind and pleasure you say *I am happy*, but those who abide in the indwelling Self beyond subject-object relationship know *I am happiness*, for the Self is happiness itself. Knowingly or unknowingly searching for happiness in all your activities are only attempts to experience that happiness of the Self, that is ever-present within you.

> *Just as a lamp illumines and reveals a pot and other objects, so also the Self (Ātmān) alone illumines the mind, sense organs, etc. These material objects by themselves cannot illumine themselves, because they are inert.*
> Shankaracharya, *Atma Bodha* 28

What is the Mind?

The *Bhāgavad Gīta 7:4* confirms that the mind is of the subtle material nature. It is one of the eight primary elements (*ashta-prakritis*): earth, water, fire, air, ether, mind, intellect and ego. In the next verse of the *Bhāgavad Gīta 7:5*, it is stated that this material nature (mind, intellect, ego) is different from the highest nature of the Self.

The mind is not self-luminous because it is a perceptible object.
Patañjali Yoga Sūtra 4:19

The mind cannot explain itself, neither can it reveal the Self (pure Consciousness), because the Self transcends the mind and intellect. The Self is always the *witness* of the mind and senses, it is always the centre in all your activities, but as an instrument the mind can help to establish the Self by logic and reasoning. When the mind is purified, disciplined and stilled, then it becomes a useful instrument; but when in ignorance it falsely identifies with the body and senses, and it becomes a source of suffering and sorrow.

The great ancient sage Patañjali, who wrote the *Yoga Sūtras*, defined the mind as waves (*vṛttis*) on the ocean of Consciousness (*citta*), and that *Yoga* (union; unity; *samādhi* – total absorption) is the stilling of those waves (*yogaś citta vṛtti nirodha*). Yoga is the absolute stilling of the mind's activity, and to achieve Yoga is to abide in one's own true nature – the changeless Self – otherwise one identifies with the ego-self and experiences duality and separateness, and is limited by the ever-changing world through the incessant activity of the mind.

The mind is so fine and subtle that it cannot be distinguished from the Consciousness, the indwelling Self. It is transparent and reflects the Consciousness without distortion, and so it is difficult to distinguish mind from the Consciousness. In its true nature, this is what the mind really is – pure mind, filled with the luminous reflection of the pure Consciousness.

The body acts, the senses perceive, and the mind thinks and feels. The mind always functions in conjunction with the sense organs, without which neither forms nor thoughts can appear. Within all these activities the changeless 'I'-principle (the centre of life) or Consciousness is found to be present, silently witnessing and knowing every one of them. *I am the witness or knower* of the body, the senses, and the mind. Being separate from the body, senses, and mind, *I am the witnessing Consciousness in all activities* (the ultimate *Knower* or *Perceiver*). Thought and feeling must have an object but Consciousness, the witnessing Self, has none, because the 'I'-principle is experience itself, and is beyond subject-object relationship. Consciousness is always your true centre, your *Being* in all activities; it is the *knowingness* that is never parted from you; it is the *Experiencer* who witnesses and knows the transient actions, perceptions, thoughts and feelings that flow in and out of the mind.

The Seat of the Mind

The mind is the seat of internal perception, which has many different functions. The principle functions are cognition, volition, and emotion. The understanding mind and intellect are all in the subtle body; they operate through corresponding centres in the physical brain. But the brain is *not* the mind; it is like a screen on which consciousness is reflected. The outer mind has its seat in the brain, through which it gains its experiences through the senses.

The inner subtle mind pervades throughout the body, but it has three main places in which it resides during the states of waking, deep sleep and dream. In the waking state the mind resides at the eyebrow centre in the *ājñā chakra*. During deep sleep the mind resides in a subtle state in the heart, *anāhata chakra*. In dream it resides in the throat, *viśuddha chakra*. In dreamless sleep there are no thoughts; the distracting world of duality temporarily disappears. As soon as you awaken from deep and dreamless sleep, you, the real Self, continue to exist. You feel you existed even during deep sleep, because consciousness is continuous.

It is in the dreamless sleep state that we get a taste of the nature of absolute bliss. It is only the mind that creates differences, sorrow, duality, and separateness.

The inner mind or feeling nature is located in the heart.

Mind, thoughts and feelings

The mind, coloured by countless latent tendencies, comes to depend on things other than itself owing to interactions with them.
Patañjali Yoga Sūtra 4:24

All objects, thoughts and feelings are known through the mind, but when these are absent, the mind cannot be said to exist. That which is existing beyond the mind is Consciousness, the changeless all-witnessing 'I'-principle. Thoughts rise in Consciousness, exist in Consciousness and disappear in Consciousness, beyond the mind. When Consciousness is limited or objectified then it is called thought. Just as waves are made of water, so thoughts are pure Consciousness.

Thoughts and feelings are like pictures projected on the background screen of the Self. To see the Self or Reality, the presence of thoughts and feelings must disappear, so that the mind is still.

We know that when the mind thinks, thoughts are constantly flowing in the mind. Whenever there are thoughts the mind comes into existence, and when there are no thoughts the mind ceases to exist. We also know that when our thoughts are calm, the mind is also calm. When the thoughts are restless the mind is restless. In other words the mind is coloured by the thoughts flowing through it.

This is like the relationship between water and a river. A pool of water is not a river, but when the water is flowing in a continuous stream it becomes a river. Similarly, thought alone is not the mind. It is only when the thoughts are flowing that we can say that the mind exists. We can take this analogy further by saying that when the waters are flowing rapidly (as over rapids) the river is in a restless state. Similarly, as the thoughts become restless with desires, so the mind becomes restless. If the thoughts are negative the mind becomes negative. Just as a cloth dipped in coloured dye takes on the colour in which it is dipped, so does the mind take on the qualities of the thoughts.

Mind, reason, will, ego – The four functions of the mind

The word 'mind' is generally used in Western psychology to signify the operation of the psyche, including memory, understanding, willing and feeling, but in Yoga psychology, there is a significantly deeper and more detailed analysis.

Just as we have five perceiving faculties: hearing, sight, smell, taste and touch to perceive the external gross manifestation of the world, so we also have the subtler functions working from within.

According to Yoga philosophy there are four aspects or functions of the mind – *manas*, *buddhi*, *ahaṁkāra* and *citta* – together they are termed as *antaḥkaraṇa* (*antah* means internal; *karana* means instrument), the 'internal instrument', located in the subtle body. The physical body acts under the direction of the *antaḥkaraṇa*, establishing contact with the physical senses to relate with the physical world of objects. It is through this internal instrument that you sense, perceive, and reason. In Yoga psychology it is called *citta*. The interaction of *citta* with *manas*, *buddhi*, and *ahaṁkāra* collectively form the *antaḥkaraṇa*. The Sanskrit words '*manas*' and '*citta*' do not translate as 'mind'; they have a broader meaning.

These four aspects of the mind – *manas*, *buddhi*, *ahaṁkāra* and *citta* – interact with the subtle organs associated with sense perception (*jñānendriyas*) and the subtle organs associated with action (*karmendriyas*), and create in us the feeling and experience of being separate.

Antaḥkaraṇa – its four functions

Manas (faculty of indeterminate knowledge; that part of the mind that receives impressions through the senses from the external world, but does not come to a final determination; deliberation. It has the ability to notice, cognise and objectify). *Manas* is centred in the head.

Buddhi (intellect; intelligence; discriminating or determinative faculty that contains intuitive wisdom. Knowledge becomes certain or determinate. It has the ability to comprehend, discern and decide). *Buddhi* is centred in the frontal brain between the eyebrows.

Ahaṁkāra (identifying faculty; ego; the sense of 'I' or personal identity). *Ahaṁkāra* is centred in the medulla oblongata of the lower brain.

Citta (the totality of the mind; field of consciousness that includes the three cognitive functions: *buddhi*, *ahaṁkāra* and *manas*; mind; *citta* stores impressions and experiences. It has the ability to remember, retain and retrieve). *Citta* is centred in the heart.

All these four faculties of the *antaḥkaraṇa* are made from subtle unconscious matter. By themselves they are all devoid of consciousness; they are insentient. It is the reflected light of the Self (Pure Consciousness) on the mind and senses that enlivens them to function. It is like the light of the Sun which reveals itself to us directly and also reveals any object that its rays of light fall on. The mind receives the light of consciousness, and because of that appears to have the power of feeling. But it is not the mind that feels, it is the Self feeling through the mind. It is the light of consciousness that enables the mind to feel. Without cognition, or consciousness, there cannot be any feeling or willing. Both feeling and willing presuppose consciousness.

The sense organs cannot perceive their respective objects unless the mind is joined with them. Again, it is the Self that is permeated with the light of consciousness that perceives the object through the mind and the sense organs. It is because of this borrowed light of consciousness that the mind proves to be the main instrument of cognition.

A way of understanding the *antaḥkaraṇa's* functions is to imagine an object at some distance under a large tree. You are unable to see the object clearly because it is in the dark shade of the tree. Your *antaḥkaraṇa* cognises the object but is unable to determine what the object really is. "What is that? Is it a person sitting under the tree, a bear, or a rock?" When the *antaḥkaraṇa* has this vacillating cognition or function of deliberation it is referred to as *manas* (the thinking mind). Then you search within and recall some past impression that is related or similar to it. With this recollection you cognise the object as a bear. This faculty of reasoning (determinative faculty) to determine the true object is *buddhi*, which is usually inadequately translated as intellect. The function of recollection and memory is *citta*. This leads to the recognition of the object, and you determine "that is a bear (sitting under the tree)." With the ascertainment "that is a bear" arises the knowledge: "I know the bear." When there is a factor of separation, for example when you are aware of being an individual different from everyone and everything else, that is called *ahaṁkāra* or ego.

In order to know something new you have to relate it to something already known. These four functions: *manas*, *buddhi*, *citta* and *ahaṁkāra* represent four different states of mind (*antaḥkaraṇa*).

Manas

Manas (from *man*, to think) is the 'instrument of thinking' or the outer mind, that includes the senses, emotions and outer thinking capacity. It interacts with the external world and takes in sensory impressions and data. The senses (*indriyas*) perceive an external object and present it to the *manas*, who considers it and then presents it to the ego (*ahaṁkāra*), who appropriates it and presents it to the intellect or intelligence (*buddhi*), thereby illuminating the purpose of the *puruṣa* (the pure, eternal, and unchanging Consciousness). The rays of *puruṣa* reflect on *buddhi* like the sun reflects on the moon or on a mirror.

Manas or the mind transmits consciousness to the body, without which the organs of perception and the body cannot function.

Manas or the mind is the most important instrument in the human personality, and is the greatest instrument of knowledge and action. All development depends on the mind. It is through concentration of the mind that you gain knowledge, and unless you concentrate your mind you will not be able to know anything.

Manas is the transmitter of consciousness, it receives the light of consciousness which gives it the power of feeling. This makes the mind look as if it has consciousness in itself, that it is self-luminous, but, actually, it is the Self that feels through the mind. The light of the Self is reflected on the mind. Just as a film projector shines light upon a screen and makes the images look real to us, and makes us identify with the feelings acted by the actors on the screen which are only light and recorded sound. Similarly, it is not actually the mind that feels, imagines, wills, hopes or fears; it is the light of the Self, of Consciousness, that enables the mind to feel and will.

Buddhi

Buddhi (from *budh*, 'to wake up', 'be aware of') is the intellect; the higher mind or intelligence that discriminates and makes decisions. *Buddhi* has the power of reason, the power to distinguish between the apparent and the false, between right and wrong, the eternal and the non-eternal, and between the Self and the non-self. The cognitive mind (*buddhi*) is the most important aspect of *citta*, because through its function of discrimination one can achieve liberation.

Buddhi is the finest of all the aspects of the mind, and being closest to the Self, reflects the radiance of consciousness. The light of the Self or Consciousness reflects in the *buddhi* (intellect); just as a clear crystal appears to take on the colour of the object upon which it rests, the pure crystal-like Self appears to take on the qualities of the *sattva-rajas-tamas guṇas*, but actually it is only *buddhi* (intellect) that takes on the condition of the *guṇas* (qualities of matter). When the crystal is removed, its own clarity becomes visible without any colouring.

Through false identification, the Self sees its reflection in the mirror of *buddhi*; it identifies with the reflected image and thinks that it is experiencing what *buddhi* is experiencing, and so forgets its true nature. The sense of 'I-ness' is transmitted to *buddhi* that starts it functioning as a conscious principle.

Ahaṁkāra

When the mind takes on the feeling of 'I-ness', and 'my-ness' it is called *ahaṁkāra*, the individual ego, which feels itself to be distinct, a separate entity. *Ahaṁkāra's* nature is to self-assert – "I am the form" and "I am the doer." *Aham* literally means 'I', as undivided Consciousness, and *Akara* means a shape or form. In this sense, *Ahaṁkāra* means the formless unlimited Consciousness that appears as a form with limitations.

> *The abandonment of ego-sense is the cessation of ignorance; this and nothing else is liberation.*
> Sage Vasiṣṭha, *Vasiṣṭha's Yoga* by Swami Venkatesananda, State University of New York Press, Albany, USA, 1993

It is difficult for us to give up this sense of 'I' because the mind is dependent; it always attaches itself to something objective. For example, the moment we have the sense of 'I' we also have the sense of I am this, I am that, I am the other thing. I cannot think of myself as the pure 'I' in this present state. The mind reflects on some condition and it says, "I am happy," or "I am sad." The ego continually moves between identification with the body ("I am a man" or "I am a woman") and identification with thoughts such as "I am beautiful", "I am intelligent".

The 'I' identifies itself either with the function of *manas* or *buddhi*; it does not seem to have any function of its own.

Ahaṁkāra conditions the *puruṣa* consciousness as the ego, with a subjective sense of self as 'I', an objectified sense of self as 'me', and appropriates through 'mine'. The ego-self causes the real Self to appear as identical with things that are not self – the mind, body, and senses, and their associated experiences. *Ahaṁkāra* consequently reduces the freedom and joy of the real Self to the ego defined condition. The personal pronoun 'I' always denotes the true Self, in which the totality of objective experience seems to occur. "I think" really means "*I am conscious of* thoughts"; and "I am happy" means "*I am conscious of a feeling* of happiness". (The mind says, "I am happy," but the Self is happiness itself.)

The ego structure is dualistic; it divides the unity of Reality into opposites and contrasting pairs. *Ahaṁkāra* as the body-mind structure is the limitation that creates the illusion of a *separate* consciousness. It is our mistaken personal identification to the body, thoughts and feelings that keeps us in ignorance of our real nature. The body, thoughts and feelings that produce a feeling of a personal self are continually changing, but we who claim them as our own are changeless. This ignorance causes us to personify the ego as our real Self. The ego sees and believes itself to be a personal, separate entity and the inferred source of its own existence. The ego seizes for its own use the existence-consciousness-happiness aspects of the real Self ('I'-principle) and claims them along also with the witnessing function to itself in all its activities. The ego says: "I perceive", "I think", "I feel", "I do" and "I know". And when the ego remembers a past thought, the real Self or 'I'-principle witnesses it.

The ego fears dissolution and therefore resists giving up the illusion of a separate existence. When ego (*ahaṁkāra)* dissolves, both oneself and the world are experienced as appearing in the One Consciousness.

Citta

Cit means 'to perceive', 'be conscious'. The 'inner mind' or consciousness is termed as *citta*. It is the mental faculty that gives us awareness and makes us feel that we exist. It includes *manas*, *buddhi* and *ahaṁkāra*. The *citta* field of consciousness or field of experience is like a memory bank which stores impressions and experiences. It stores our thoughts, feelings, likes and dislikes. All present actions, past memories and visions of the future take place in *citta*.

Citta is a comprehensive term, and like the word *manas*, it may represent the whole of the mind. In Raja Yoga *citta* is usually termed as 'mind field' or 'field of consciousness'. It is within this field of consciousness that all present actions, past memories, and future visions take place. In Vedanta philosophy the subconscious mind is termed as *citta*.

The functions of *citta* are memory, attention, concentration, and enquiry. Sensations from the sense organs communicate themselves first to that part of the mind called *citta*. So the first effort of the mind begins with the idea of gaining happiness and fulfilment outwardly through the senses. Part of its function is the search for happiness and fulfilment.

Citta is the conscious awareness with which we identify our being; it is the mind of the soul. *Citta* dwells in the spiritual heart, which is located on the right side of the physical heart. It is in this spiritual heart that deep feeling and knowing are working. The nature of *citta* is the capacity to feel: feeling through thought, emotion, feeling, and sensation.

A thought is somehow converted into a feeling because of some 'interference' somewhere. "I like him", "I don't like him", "she looks beautiful", "she looks ugly". This judgement comes after thought formation. But where does all this take place? The material of which the sensations in their essential nature are made is *citta*. What is being said here is nothing but a string of words and more words. Yet *citta* still remains *citta*, and it will not be grasped by your mind, however intelligent you may be, until this thing that we call *citta* jumps in front of you and says: "I am *citta*." The *citta* must be as true, as real to you as your own body, or as the chair you sit on, which you can see and touch. It must be as real as an ant crawling on your leg, felt externally, or the headache or anger experienced internally.

Seeing the chair is a perception of a material object. Being aware of a crawling ant on your leg is a sensation, and the feeling of anger is an emotion. In one or all of these contexts the *citta* must become visible to you. You must *experience* it. It must be an existential, immediate reality for you. Not, "I think once I experienced the self, or had direct vision of the *citta*." If you had a headache six years ago, you cannot reproduce that same feeling now. No mother can relive the labour pains she had at the time of childbirth.

All the things we call meditation, *citta*, *vṛtti*, control (*nirodha*) etc are irrelevant now, in terms of the *now*. These things do not mean anything to you here and now unless they actually exist in you at present. Just as you cannot experience a headache that is not actually there in you, you cannot meditate unless there *is* meditation, you cannot know what *citta* is unless *citta* reveals itself to you. You can do nothing about it. Until it happens, until life becomes intolerable to you, until all your desires, all your cravings begin to hurt you and the mind naturally turns upon itself, the understanding will not be there.

One cannot be false unto oneself. Only when it hurts will the mind detach from the cravings, the lust, the greed, and the hatred. You do not have to detach from them at all. When you have developed sensitivity within yourself, then without any outside persuasion, the mind is ready to let them drop. Then the *citta* is seen, is experienced.

Meditation is coming face to face with *citta*. In that state of *Yoga* in which there is an inner understanding of the *vṛttis* and the *citta*. When this meditation, *Yoga*, takes place, then the *citta* has turned upon itself. The *citta* has become itself, and it remains in its own purity without any distortion whatsoever.

Five Conditions of the Mind (*Citta*)

1. *mūḍha* (dull and preoccupied; stupefied)
2. *kṣipta* (restless; disturbed)

3. *vikṣipta* (distracted)
4. *ekāgra* (one-pointed)
5. *niruddha* (restrained; controlled)

These five conditions of the mind or *citta* (field of consciousness) can be classified under two main states: the controlled and the uncontrolled. The dysfunctional uncontrolled conditions of the mind or *citta* are: *mūḍha*, *kṣipta*, and *vikṣipta*. The controlled are *ekāgra* and *niruddha*. In the *Yoga Sūtras* 1:2 of the great Sage, Patañjali, he states that *Yoga* is the control and stilling of the vortices of feeling that swirl in eddies around the thoughts in the mind (*Yogaś citta vṛtti nirodha*).

Uncontrolled states of the mind

Mūḍha – When the mind is predominated by the quality of *tamas guṇa* it becomes inert, dull, dark and stupefied due to worry, hopelessness, dejection and grief.

Kṣipta – The predominance of *rajas guṇa* causes the mind to become disturbed and restless with desire, anger, fear and doubt, causing total unsteadiness.

Vikṣipta – In the distracted state the quality of *sattva guṇa* (illumination) begins to predominate but there is still some *rajas* and *tamas* activity, which causes the mind to be distracted.

The nine 'distractors of the mind'

There are nine 'distractors of the mind' (*citta vikṣepa*) which are obstacles to Yoga or Self-realisation. Patañjali lists them in his *Yoga Sūtras* (1:30) as:

1. **Disease or illness** (*vyādhi*) – Disease or illness distracts your attention.
2. **Dullness** (*styāna*) – Mental inertia and procrastination. A lack of a sense of purpose. Lacking interest and enthusiasm

in your daily routines and spiritual practices.

3. **Doubt** (*saṁśaya*) – Doubt is your worst enemy. When the mind is in doubt it becomes undecided, uncertain, and even disbelieving. Through lack of conviction and self-confidence, doubt arises and disturbs your inner attention and inner peace. You are then unable to keep your mind focused and to turn it inward.
4. **Carelessness** (*pramāda*) – Carelessness and negligence is failing to be constantly attentive, and being uninterested in your spiritual practices and disciplines. It is a lack of persistent effort.
5. **Laziness** (*ālasya*) – Inertia from physical and mental heaviness feeds laziness caused by lack of discipline, willingness and enthusiasm.
6. **Inability to withdraw the mind from sense cravings** (*avirati*) – Desire and craving for sense-gratification and attachment to worldly pleasures and objects. The senses become unrestrained and indulgence becomes an unconscious involvement of the senses with the objects of the world. The desire for objects creates greed and also the fear of losing the desired objects. A mind lost in desire, greed and fear is incapable of comprehending and experiencing reality as it is. It blocks divine grace and thwarts our spiritual development.
7. **Delusion** (*bhrānti-darśana*) – Deluded ideas and misconceptions about the Yoga methods or the spiritual path itself.
8. **Non-achievement of a Yogic state** (*alabdha-bhumikatva*) – Inability to practise and maintain concentration. Failure to attain any stage of *samādhi* (superconsciousness).
9. **Instability** (*an-avasthitatvāni*) – Restlessness of the mind due to distractions. A stage of *samādhi* has been attained but the mind is unstable and so it is not established in the superconscious state.

These nine obstacles or 'distractors of the mind' (*citta vikṣepa*) can be narrowed down to basically three main categories: **dullness**, **unsteadiness** and **ignorance**. Accompanying these nine obstacles are five symptoms that distract the mind:

> *Pain, frustration, mental agitation, unsteadiness of limbs, erratic breathing in or out are the accompanying distractions.*
> Patañjali Yoga Sūtra 1:31

Pain (*duḥkha*) gives rise to mental agitation and restlessness from unfulfilled desires. The obstacles: illness, inertia and doubt bring unhappiness, giving rise to dejection, and the powerful emotions of anger, fear and grief. These negative feelings make the mind unsteady and we lose our confidence in the ability to overcome the problems. We then become doubtful and unsteady not only in our mind but also in our body, our nervous system becomes disturbed, and breathing becomes erratic.

Pain (*duḥkha*) is classified in three different ways:

> *Ādhyātmika* (within oneself) – physical disease and illness, mental and emotional pain caused by negative emotions.
> *Ādhibautika* (caused by other beings) – pain resulting from external causes including insects, snakes and animals.
> *Ādhidaivika* (caused by natural elemental forces) – natural disasters such as earthquakes, floods, fires, and planetary forces.

The means to remove the obstacles and transform the mind

The means and methods to remove the causes and conditions of inner unrest, the obstacles or impediments (*antarāya*), and to transform the mind, are through the practice of *abhyāsa* (persistent practice) and *vairāgya* (non-attachment) (Yoga Sūtras 1:12), meditation (Yoga Sūtras 1:32), and by the grace of *Īśvara*, the inner guide and source of inspiration (Yoga Sūtras 1:29).

Controlled states of the mind

Ekāgra – When the mind is pure and has clarity and peacefulness it has the illuminating power of *sattva guṇa*. The mind then being stable can flow calmly inward, and superconsciousness with perfect wisdom (*saṁprajñāta samādhi*) can develop.

Niruddha – The steady, calm, and peaceful clear mind, being perfectly controlled, can focus on its luminous nature. The mental consciousness turns inward to become aware of its Source. With the *guṇas* dissolved, the Self becomes established in its own true nature. This is the state called *asaṁprajñāta samādhi*.

The Restless Mind

In the sixth chapter of the *Bhāgavad Gīta* (6:34), on the subject of meditation, Arjuna realises deep within himself that the mind cannot be stilled, and he says to Krishna, "the mind is restless, turbulent, strong and unyielding, I find it as difficult to control as the wind."

Krishna answers:

O Mighty-armed Arjuna, without doubt, the mind is restless and difficult to control; but by practice (abhyāsa) and by dispassion (vairāgya) it is restrained.
Bhāgavad Gīta 6:35

The mind's turbulence shows not only the speed in the flow of thoughts but also their restlessness and agitations. It is like a strong and powerful wind creating turbulence over the sea, causing uneven waves to rise and fall on the surface of the water.

When the mind is turbulent it is very difficult to calm, and when it becomes strongly attached to the objects of the senses or to a strong emotional feeling, or a negative thought, it is difficult to pull it or turn it away from its attachments. Also, if the mind has flown like the wind into a channel of its own choice, for the moment it is so unyielding that it is impossible to pull it back from its flight and persuade it to stay at the determined point of concentration.

In Chapter Three of the *Bhāgavad Gīta* (3.36), Arjuna asks this question: *"By what is one impelled, even against his will, to do wrong, constrained as it were by force?"*

We may also ask, what is it that makes the mind go astray? Why should it behave like this?

> *By dwelling on the sense objects a person develops an attachment to them. From attachment arises desire, and when desire is obstructed anger arises. From anger arises delusion. And from delusion comes forgetfulness of the Self, and from loss of memory comes the loss of the faculty of discrimination, resulting in annihilation of all right understanding.*
> Bhāgavad Gīta 2:62–63

Krishna gives this answer: *"It is* ***desire****; it is* ***anger****, both of which are impelled by rajoguṇa"* (quality of activity or passion). Desire and anger are related, because desire itself under certain circumstances gains expression as anger. Desire is a constant agitation of the mind, expressing as an uncontrollable impatience to gain something or someone. When desire gets obstructed from attaining its desired object, frustration arises because the desire is unable to be fulfilled. Unsatisfied with the unfulfilled desire to obtain the object or person causes anger. When the powerful and violent force of anger arises it gives us no time to discriminate, our memory wavers and we forget to discriminate wisely. This leads to the loss of reason and the forgetfulness of our true nature as the Self, resulting in a completely imbalanced mind.

Without pure reason one is unable to discriminate the truth from non-truth, the real from the unreal, the eternal from non-eternal.

Desires and attachment

Attachment is that which accompanies (the remembrance of) pleasure.
Patañjali Yoga Sūtra 2:7

Ignorance (*avidyā*) is the cause of egoism (*asmitā*) and egoism gives rise to attachment (*rāga*). The Sanskrit word *rāga* comes from *raj* (to be excited) and can mean desire, attraction or attachment. For attachment to arise, memory is required. When you eat a delicious Italian ice cream and enjoy the pleasurable taste sensations of it, your mind immediately stores the memory of that pleasurable sensation and desires another experience of the same pleasure. This creates an attachment (*moha*), a desire to achieve pleasure (*sukha*) and possess the object of desire. The ice cream (or any insentient object, or a sentient person) is *not* the source of pleasure or happiness. If you were to eat six ice creams immediately one after the other, do you think that would give you the same pleasure, satisfaction and happiness as if you only ate one ice cream? No, your stomach would feel full, bloated and uncomfortable. You would soon lose the pleasurable feeling and emotional satisfaction, and begin to feel pain (*duḥkha*) instead.

To a person of discrimination all worldly experience is painful. Change causes anxiety and fear, pleasure reinforces latent tendencies (vāsanās) to recreate new desires, and also because the opposing nature of the guṇas (forces of nature – sattva, rajas and tamas that control the mind) counteract one another.
Patañjali Yoga Sūtra 2:15

If you believe that the feeling of pleasure and your happiness comes from the ice cream, or any other object that you may be attracted to (including a person), your mind will always seek satisfaction outside itself. The wise know that in every pleasure is its opposite, pain, and that in the seeking of pleasure and the attachment to pleasure, both create pain.

We need to remember that pleasure and happiness are *not* the same. Pleasure is a fleeting momentary joy experienced through the senses, whereas true happiness is the outcome of the inner state of tranquillity. The moment the pleasurable object or pleasurable experience disappears, the pleasure we derive from it disappears as well. Then the absence, memory, and attachment to the object of pleasure cause us mental pain. The mind becomes unsteady and unstable; it is not able to remain calm, peaceful and content.

When we are preoccupied only with seeking pleasure through sense-gratification, then there is a loss of will and desire to know the Truth, the reality of our true essential nature as the blissful, peaceful Self within us. The mind becomes dissipated and a slave to the senses. With such an unrestrained mind there can be no inner peace, no true happiness and joy, and no spiritual fulfilment or success in concentration and meditation. It is only when your mind, senses, action and speech are disciplined, mastered, and directed toward the spiritual goal that you can attain inner and outer freedom.

Beyond pleasure and pain

We all want to avoid pain, but most of us seek pleasure not realising that the pursuit of pleasure only brings more pain. To go beyond the duality of both pain and pleasure is to use discriminative wisdom to realise your true nature of the indwelling eternal blissful Self, which is *Sat-Cit-Ānanda* (ever-existent, ever-conscious, ever-new Bliss). The indwelling Self, which has no duality, is beyond the mind-body complex and *guṇas* (forces of nature – *sattva*, *rajas*, and *tamas*); it has no experience of the changes of pain or pleasure. Pain and pleasure are only experiences of the mind not of the inner Self. To go beyond pleasure and pain do not seek it, neither avoid it, but abide in your true essential nature as the blissful Self.

Pain that can appear in the future is avoidable.
Patañjali Yoga Sūtra 2:16

The Sanskrit word for pain, sorrow or misery is *duḥkha*. The great Sage Patañjali tells us that the cause of suffering is avoidable. We can prevent pain, sorrow and misery before it even comes to us, by discriminative wisdom. Through the disciplined and steady practices of Yoga and meditation the aspirant prevents future pain and misery. Pain is experienced in the objectified mind, so to go beyond pain you need to abide in the subjective, changeless, all-knowing, witnessing Self. This means identifying with your true essential nature, the inner Self, and not identifying with the changing body, the individual I-sense in the intellect (*buddhi*), nor the ego (*ahaṁkāra*) for that is not who you are. That is not your real identity.

Why do desires arise in us? And where do they arise from?
Due to forgetfulness of our real spiritual nature, our true Source of life, which is ever-conscious, ever-present, ever-new Bliss (*Sat-Cit-Ānanda*), we remain in ignorance (*avidyā*) of our eternal, divine God-Self that is within us. Through false identification we identify ourselves with the non-self, and with all that keeps our mind externally preoccupied. Our forgetfulness is not total; and it is because of this that we cling to existence. God, or our own divine Self, is infinite Being. Even if our mind forgets, the Self that illumines the mind is ever-conscious and ever-present. And so we cling to life, as that is what *being* means to us; we all fear annihilation or death. You, the spiritual Self, are an infinite *being* expressing as life through your material, physical mind, body and senses. All the negative and positive impulses that arise within you – desires, emotions and feelings – can be traced either to affirming your true nature or denial of it. Your true *being* is infinite, but if anything in your experience seems to take away from the infinity of your being, then you resist, hate, or fear it. Through erroneously identifying

ourselves with the material mind-body we think that our happiness and joy comes from adding more to it, so we become preoccupied with sense-gratification and the pleasures derived from the objects of the senses. There is also a sense of wanting expansion of being to increase our joy, so what do we do? We add another body to us, we form a relationship, marry, and create a family, or we join a social network and gather lots of friends to us. The more we gain materially gives us a greater sense of expansion, but because it is all on the material level and concerned with the mind-body complex, it cannot be real and everlasting. For all that is born materially of this world is impermanent and will eventually leave us and pass away. Desire for and attachment to what is impermanent causes pain and sorrow. Desires from which thoughts continuously flow into the mind disturb the reflection of the Truth in it.

As we continue through life with our preoccupation of gratifying our senses, seeking pleasure through our endless desires, and even seeking worldly knowledge, in trying to seek an everlasting happiness, some of us come to a point in our lives when we begin to think that something is missing. Desires arise from our search from our own infinite Divinity, our true eternal nature, the God-Self within. Outwardly, in the world we are all seeking truth, knowledge, love, peace, beauty, and a joy or bliss that is everlasting! All these attributes belong to our true nature, the inner Self (*Sat-Cit-Ānanda*). Everyone wants to abide in their own true blissful nature, their own Truth, but due to forgetfulness of our spiritual nature, we became convinced that the fundamental reality is material, so we erroneously started to realise this infinite *Being* through matter, and therefore it became distorted.

Your thoughts develop your character

Your thoughts develop your character and create your destiny:

Sow a *thought* and reap a *character*,
Sow an *action* and reap a *habit*,

Sow a *habit* and reap a *character*,
Sow a *character* and reap a *destiny*.

Your present character is an index of your previous thoughts, and the present state of your experience is due to the thoughts, feelings and actions of your past lives. You mould your destiny from within by your own thoughts and actions. Your thoughts are the architect of the circumstances you encounter; they build your life. So you need to be constantly vigilant, because every thought creates a vibration in your mental body, which is transmitted to your physical body and nervous system. When you dwell on a particular thought a vibration is set up and established. The vibration of this thought continues to repeat itself; it becomes automatic and creates a habit. Thoughts gain power and strength by repetition; the more you entertain a thought, either good or bad, the more its vibration will resonate in your mind and recur. So discriminate wisely in the use of your thoughts. Be indifferent to all negative thoughts and cultivate positive thinking.

If you introspect and watch your mind with awareness, you will notice that many thoughts that arise are inconsistent, and that your mind wanders aimlessly. When a thought arises in your mind, enquire: "Why has this thought arisen? Whom does it concern? Who am I?"

Affirm: "I am not the mind. I am *Sat-Cit-Ānanda* (ever-Existent, ever-Conscious, ever-new Bliss). I am pure Consciousness, the changeless, eternal blissful Self. I am the Experiencer and Witness of these thoughts, feelings and emotions." Then by internalising your mind to its Source, the mental activity, the thoughts and emotions will cease. Rise above your thoughts and abide in your real essential nature, the inner Self, which is pure Consciousness where there are no thoughts and no disturbance, only stillness.

The fewer the desires you have, the lesser the thoughts, and the fewer the thoughts you have the greater your mental strength, concentration and inner peace.

> *When the mind is disturbed by negative thoughts one should cultivate opposite (positive) thoughts.*
> Patañjali Yoga Sūtra 2:33

Obstacles that obstruct your Self-awareness arise because of negative thoughts, habits and tendencies that were formed by the latent *saṁskāras* of past actions. By encouraging and affirming positive thoughts, negative tendencies are opposed and weakened. For example if you have a bad habit of thinking negatively, and anger arises in your mind, then cultivate its opposite of compassion. If your thoughts are hateful, then cultivate loving thoughts. If you have deceitful thoughts then cultivate honesty.

Habits

> *Change the trend of your thoughts – cast out all negative mental habits. Replace them with wholesome, courageous thought habits, and apply them in daily life with unshakable confidence.*
> Paramhansa Yogananda, *How to Be a Success: The Wisdom of Yogananda, Volume 4*, Crystal Clarity Publishers, Nevada City, CA, 2008

The lives of most persons are not governed by weak resolutions, but by habits. These lifetime habits are ingrained in us; they create imbalance and disharmony within us. Habits also create addictions, that temporarily give us a sense of comfort, but ultimately they disempower us; we lose our wise discrimination and willpower. Addiction is a symptom of a much deeper problem that a person struggles to deal with and suffers from. An addictive pattern can be a long and difficult process to get out of.

A habit is an acquired habitual behaviour, thought pattern, or old belief that one repeats so many times that it becomes almost unconscious. The behaviour is so ingrained in us that we act without thinking about what we are saying or doing. Most of the time we engage in habits without thinking, which can either be helpful or harmful. In a positive and beneficial sense the formation of a good habit enables you to act automatically on 'autopilot', freeing up time and energy for you to focus on other things that need your special attention. In a negative sense bad habits can cause problems in your personal life and affect others. They can cause mental and physical ill health, they waste time and energy, and they prevent you from accomplishing your worthy goals in life.

These bad habits are not only the obvious habits, such as habitually biting your nails, eating the wrong foods or overeating, or smoking, but include psychological or mental bad habits such as procrastination, gossiping, thinking negatively, resisting change, negatively criticising and being judgemental toward others.

Changing negative habits

To overcome a bad habit the first thing you need to do is ask yourself: What is missing from life? What gap in my life am I trying to fill by doing this habit? Is boredom, loneliness or stress a factor involved? Or is there something deeper that is causing you to hold on to something that is bad for you? Perhaps a fear, an event, or a limiting belief?

Some deeply rooted habits or beliefs may take longer to eliminate from your consciousness. This habitual energy that has lingered from the past can resurface and throw you off balance, distracting and stressing you. Remember that you have come to your present condition through errors and mistakes lasting lifetimes, so do not expect in one day, or one week, or even one month to root out old beliefs and old and tenacious bad habits, and break free from the cyclic force of habitual activity. It can take time to destroy old habits and replace them with new fresh ideas, creating good habits. If you are to conquer the foe of bad habits that drive you to act in ways to maintain suffering, then you must banish them completely from the kingdom of your mind, and establish the rightful ruler, the indwelling divine Self, on the throne to guide you with wisdom and understanding. This is where you will need self-discipline, commitment to practise (*abhyāsa*), non-attachment, dispassion (*vairāgya*), patience, willpower, and a strong persistent perseverance, willingness and resolve to succeed. Then gradually you will find that the positive and good habits will begin to influence your life in a beneficial way, and on all levels – physical, mental and spiritual.

Methods of overcoming bad habits

To weaken an old or bad habit avoid everything that arouses and stimulates it. Divert the attention of your mind toward a good positive habit, and cultivate it by the strength of your willpower and the power of deep concentration. In other words, neutralise bad habits by creating good habits. Meditate daily to erase the pattern of old and bad habits.

Sit quietly and peacefully in a seated meditation posture that is comfortable for you, with your head, neck and spine aligned upright. Then, centring yourself within, relax and free your mind from all worries and restlessness. Then pray:

> *Heavenly Father, grant me the wisdom to discriminate wisely. Strengthen my willpower to conquer and defeat all wrong tendencies and bad habits in me. May Your Divine Light reveal the errors in my consciousness and dissolve them completely. Lead me from the darkness of ignorance to the Light of Your Supreme Consciousness in Truth and eternal Joy.*

Now concentrating deeply at the command centre (*Ājñā Chakra* – midpoint between the eyes on the forehead), meditate for a few minutes. Then using any of the affirmations below, with firm intention and sincerity, say it first aloud, then softly, then fading into a whisper, and finally affirm mentally with faith and conviction, so that the affirmation carries its meaning deep down into the subconscious:

As I follow my true inner wisdom and guidance I identify false, harmful, and destructive habits, and drive them out of my mind, and change what needs to be changed. I now release old patterns, habits, and beliefs and replace them with fresh new positive thoughts. I am strong, confident and courageous to overcome all useless thoughts and habits. I let go and release from my consciousness all that is not needed. As I let go of old binding habits I make space in my consciousness to fill it with positive, wise, and divine thoughts and ideas that help me to grow in understanding, love, wisdom and truth. I experience true freedom as I awaken to my spiritual nature. I hold this truth in my mind.

My mind is like a garden; I uproot the weeds of bad thoughts and bad habits and eliminate them. Creating space in my mind-garden, I plant and cultivate beautiful fresh and new positive thoughts and good habits. I nourish my beautiful garden of consciousness by connecting in deep meditation with the Divine Consciousness. So that blooms of love unfold their beauty and life in me.

I relax and cast aside all old patterns, habits and beliefs, allowing new positive and divine thoughts to take their place.

I am free to choose positive thoughts. I release all limiting thoughts and habits, and connect with my inner Self, that knows no limits. I let go of fear, worry, and stress, and connecting with my inner creative potential, I release all thoughts of boredom.

With awareness I learn to observe my feelings, thoughts, actions, reactions, and responses. I rise to a higher consciousness; my new perspective gives me clear direction. Divinely inspired, I soar beyond all limitations.

I release all negative thoughts, feelings and false beliefs that have formed error patterns and that have blocked the natural flow of spiritual energy in me into the Light of the indwelling Self and let them go. I now reconnect with the Light and Truth in the Divine Consciousness within me.

I turn away from all slavish habits that hold me in bondage. I connect with the sacred Presence and Source of Life and inspiration to wisely guide my thoughts from within.

The best time to repeat affirmations with deep concentration is when you awake first thing in the morning when you are feeling fresh and alert from a good night's sleep, and last thing at night just before falling asleep. At these times the subconscious mind is more receptive to receiving such positive affirmations.

Saṁskāras

Every action you perform, whether physical, verbal or mental, creates a subtle karmic impression in your mind. An action that is often repeated reinforces the impression, creating a deep groove, which is stored in the form of a memory. Mental force flows in the weak spots, in old grooves of mundane thoughts and desires. In Yoga terminology the Sanskrit word for this subtle karmic impression is *saṁskāra*. The *saṁskāras* identified as thoughts, desires, and tendencies in the mind which lead to action and reaction can be compared to a garden in which seeds have been planted. Without the right soil and weather conditions, the seeds remain dormant. Similarly, *saṁskāras* also remain dormant if they are not connected with the mind, senses and objects. As soon as a dormant seed becomes activated by the warmth of the soil and is watered by the rain, it begins to grow. Similarly, *saṁskāras* wait for an opportunity to manifest: a recollection of pleasure, a memory of a sensation from something that gave us momentary satisfaction can occupy and churn the mind. This is the latent or dormant karmic impression, a *saṁskāra*, that like a seed has been watered, has been activated and has pushed its way up into our awareness from deep within our subconscious mind. The mind becomes restless with this *saṁskāric* thought, creating desire and attachment, and forming a habit by the impulse within it to repeat the same pleasurable experience. The greater the attachment the stronger the *saṁskāra* it creates.

Vāsanās

The more powerful and deeply embedded *saṁskāras* are known as *vāsanās*, which means 'colouring'. *Vāsanās* are your unmanifested tendencies that colour the mind affecting your desires, feelings, thoughts and intentions; they shape your mind and colour it, and dominate it, and create your character and life. When this happens your thoughts, speech and actions become conditioned by your *vāsanās*. Their roots are so deeply embedded in the soil of the mind that they dictate how and what you think, without you even being aware of it. A vicious cycle is set up in which thoughts to subtle karmic impressions and from subtle karmic impressions to thoughts continuously revolve.

It is only when these *vāsanās* are exhausted that the mind automatically becomes quiet. It is only in a quiet mind that peace and happiness is experienced. *Vāsanās* control your thoughts, which in turn create your actions. By changing your thoughts, you can change your life. When a negative thought enters your mind, immediately and totally reject it, and substitute an opposite positive thought. Never leave your mind idle, weak, or vacant. To prevent negative and useless thoughts from invading your mind, fill your mind with positive and optimistic thoughts, and creative ideas, that will create good habits to purify and transform your mind both mentally and spiritually, bringing you inner and outer fulfilment and true happiness.

Vṛttis – The subtle vortices of mental energy

When the subtle karmic impressions and the ephemeral and transitory thoughts continuously revolve and spin in the mind, causing it to be restless and agitated, they are called *vṛttis*. These mental tendencies and disturbances, that cause vortices of energy and movement in the mind, arise due to desires, attachment, likes and dislikes, fear, anger, and doubt. They are created when the reflection of the inner light of the Self reflects in the intellect, the discriminating faculty (*buddhi*), giving it the power to cognise objects and experience sensations. The *buddhi* and the Self then appear to have one single cognition and perception. The Self, the experiencer, becomes identified with the thoughts, creating the I-sense: "I am thinking" and "I am feeling". It also creates a feeling of a separate existence in us, an individual personality, and this is why we sometimes feel that although we may have everything of the world, there is still that feeling and sense of something *missing* in us.

This reflection of the Self in the intellect and the reflection of the objects in the intellect mix together and create *vṛttis*. In this way *vṛttis* serve the *buddhi* as an instrument of the indwelling Self to experience the external world, and to attain Self-realisation and liberation, the goal of Yoga.

Just as waves, whirlpools and bubbles arise on the surface of the lake, so also *vṛttis* arise on the surface of the mind-lake. In Sanskrit these ripples or waves are called *vṛtti*, from the verb root *vṛt* which means 'vortex; whirlpool, to revolve, movement'. Like waves ruffling the calm surface of a lake, the waves of feeling and thoughts disturb the calmness and peace of the mind or field of *consciousness* (*citta*). Just as the movement of wind creates waves on the surface of a lake, similarly objects (*pratyaya*) create *vṛttis* in the mind. When the wind becomes calm, the waves merge back into the water. Similarly, when the objects are removed from the mind, the waves of feeling and thoughts merge back into the *citta* (mind-field of consciousness).

Again, think of the mind as being like a lake, as memories rise like bubbles to the surface every subtle mental impression creates a ripple. These ripples begin to agitate the mind causing it to think and act. The incessant mental activities reinforce the subtle impressions (*saṁskāras*) and cause the ripples to increase in momentum, forming bigger and stronger waves.

We can also use the analogy of a clear, still lake, into which a stone has been thrown, causing ripples to disturb the calm surface. The stone represents *avidyā* (ignorance). The clear, still lake is the consciousness of *citta*. The ripples created by the stone are the *vṛttis*: the vortices of feelings and thoughts that oscillate in the consciousness of *citta* (field of consciousness; mind).

Patañjali in his *Yoga Sūtras* (1:2) calls this state: *"Citta vṛtti nirodha"*, a state in which there is no movement in Consciousness. When all the *vṛttis* cease Consciousness becomes still and crystal clear, and in that state, the Seer (*draṣṭṛi*) becomes aware of Itself. The Seer, the Knower or the Self, becomes established in its own true nature (*Yoga Sūtras* 1:3).

Conversely, if the Self becomes identified with the *vṛttis*, then it becomes mixed up with them. There is a false identification:

> *In other states (when the Self is not established in its own true divine nature), the Self assumes the forms of the mental modifications.*
> Yoga Sūtra 1:4

Yogas citta vṛtti nirodha

> Yoga (the realisation of the Self) is the neutralisation or stilling of the vortices of feeling in the mind.

The meaning of Patañjali's teaching here is that to realise the indwelling Self or pure Consciousness, one must first calm the thoughts and vortices of feeling that create the restless waves on the surface of the mind. Then one comes to the realisation that one's own mind is the universal Mind, and that one's self is the universal Self. The Self, the experiencer, the knower, is established in an unmodified state, in its own true nature. The Self remains changeless, ever pure and perfect, as the one who sees (*draṣṭuḥ*), who experiences and observes. The Self exists by itself and as itself. There is no division, no divided experience. It is not modified by the *citta* (mind), *vṛttis* (mental modifications), *vāsanās* (subtle desires) or *saṁskāras* (subtle karmic impressions). Just as the ocean always remains the ocean, even when it breaks into tempestuous waves (like *vṛttis* disturbing the mind) and breaks on to the shore, and rolls back again into the ocean, the ocean is not diminished. Ocean is always ocean and water is always water. That is its essential nature.

The cause of *Vṛttis*

Vṛttis or movements of the mind are caused by the five *Kleśas* (afflictions; impediments); these are the obstacles that stop us from realising our true nature.

> *There are five kinds of vṛttis, some are painful and some are not painful.*
> Patañjali Yoga Sūtra 1:5

> *Ignorance, egoism, attachment, aversion, and clinging to life are the five obstacles.*
> Patañjali Yoga Sūtra 2:3

The five afflictions or obstacles

1. ***Avidyā*** (ignorance)
2. ***Asmitā*** ('I-sense')
3. ***Rāga*** (attachment)
4. ***Dveṣa*** (aversion)
5. ***Abhiniveśa*** (clinging to life; fear of death)

Avidyā

> *Ignorance is regarding permanence in the impermanent, purity in the impure, pleasure in suffering, and the Self in the non-self.*
> Patañjali Yoga Sūtra 2:5

Vidyā in Sanskrit means Self-knowledge, or *adhyātma*, realising and knowing your true nature. *Avidyā* means ignorance, but not in the ordinary sense of the word meaning lacking general knowledge of the world. *Avidyā* means ignorance about one's own true nature. Ignorance here refers to wrong identification with one's body, mind, and senses. It is the identification with the sensation of the ego-self, of the 'Me' – "I am the body," "I am American," "I am Catholic," "I am a swami," "I am hurt," "This is mine!"

Asmitā

> *Egoism is identifying the power of the Seer (Puruṣa) with the instrument of seeing (buddhi).*
> Patañjali Yoga Sūtra 2:6

Asmi means 'I am'. *Asmitā* is the sense of individuality, the principle of egoism: 'I-sense', 'I-am-ness'. *Asmitā* the effect of *buddhi* evolves out of ignorance (*avidyā* – the root cause of all other *kleśas*).

Buddhi, the intelligence-awareness aspect of *citta*, is the primary instrument of *puruṣa* (the Self). Without *buddhi*, *puruṣa* would have no awareness of the *Prakṛiti* (matter; primordial nature) mind and body. *Asmitā* or the ego falsely identifies *buddhi*, the instrumental power of sight, with the *puruṣa*, the divine inner Self. In other words the ego misidentifies the changing non-self with the changeless and eternal true Self (*puruṣa*) as a result of illusion.

When the 'I-sense' becomes falsely identified as having a separate existence and self-importance, it is known as the ego (*ahaṁkāra*). Due to ignorance (*avidyā*) and our conditioned consciousness we think of ourselves as 'having' a soul, whereas in fact we are the divine Self expressing through a body-mind. The *citta-vṛtti* that wc perceive is the activity of your divine inner Self.

Egoism causes false identification with our body, mind, energy and senses, which are all subject to change and are non-eternal. This false identification causes us to say: "I am happy," "I am sad," "I am angry." This is misidentification. We are falsely identifying with our mental states, not the true Self. It is only the condition of the mind that is happy, sad, or angry. The indwelling Divine Self is beyond the emotional states of duality; it is changeless and eternal. Its nature is joy or bliss.

Rāga-Dveṣa

> *(Due to the identification with pleasurable experiences) attachment (rāga) arises with pleasure.*
> Patañjali Yoga Sūtra 2:7

> *(Due to the identification with painful experiences) aversion (dveṣa) arises with suffering.*
> Patañjali Yoga Sūtra 2:8

In its separation the ego experiences 'likes' and 'dislikes' – objects or persons appear either as attractive (*rāga*) or repulsive (*dveṣa*) to the ego-self. There is approval and disapproval. *Rāga*, which also means attachment, arises every time the mind recollects any type of pleasure or happiness connected with an object or person. Memory precedes attachment. It is the past impressions called *saṁskāras* that remain latent in the mind, causing it and the senses to be subconsciously pulled toward objects and persons that have given pleasurable experiences in the past.

Dveṣa or aversion and dislike felt for an object or person arises from the memory of pain or unhappiness connected with an object or person. Attachment and aversion keep us continually bound to the limited level of mundane consciousness. They strengthen the ego, creating an unending flow of desires and habits that condition our behaviour, which in turn conceals the bliss of our true nature.

Abhiniveśa

> *The fear of separation by death from the body is inherent in both the ignorant and the wise.*
> Patañjali Yoga Sūtra 2:9

The fifth *kleśa*, clinging to life and fear of death (*abhiniveśa*), is the tenacious clinging to life, not wanting to let go of the ego, which is resistant to change. Clinging to life is the habit of dependence on objective sources of enjoyment and happiness, and fear of losing them. This clinging to life is inherent in us all, including the wise not only the ignorant, because latent within us are the stronger *saṁskāra* seed-impressions of death. It can only be completely eradicated by transcending the identification with being an individual. The greatest fear is death, fearing that we will cease to exist and lose our identity.

Due to ignorance (*avidyā*) the ego-self, the 'I', identifies with the mind-body and believes that the 'I' dies when the body dies. But the 'I', the true Divine Self which is of the nature of Spirit, is eternal, it cannot die. Anything that is not self-luminous, nor self-aware, and does not have consciousness as its very essence, is non-eternal. Both the mind and the body are of a material nature that is subject to change, and therefore cannot be eternal. Though the mind is of a material nature, it is very subtle and can reflect the consciousness of the Self or Spirit. Consciousness is not inherent in the mind so it borrows the light of consciousness from the Self.

How to overcome the five afflictions (*Kleśas*)

> *These subtle afflictions are eliminated by resolving them back into their original cause.*
> Patañjali Yoga Sūtra 2:10

The afflictions have their roots in ignorance (*avidyā*), which is their primal cause, and are not easily eliminated or destroyed. Even though the afflictions can be resolved back into their primal cause, if ignorance remains in any form, there is still the potential for the afflictions to return to their fully active states. It is only when one attains the perfection of *asamprajñāta samādhi* in *nirvikalpa-samādhi*, the final liberation (*kaivalya*), that there is complete freedom from the afflictions (*kleśas*).

If we use an analogy of a tree, our desires are like the leaves, twigs and branches. The branches are the strong central desires that branch out into less stronger or weaker desires (desires that are known) in the twigs and leaves. The afflictions – ignorance, egoism, attraction, repulsion and clinging to life – are the roots of the tree and trunk of the tree. It is not enough to only remove the numerous leaves, to reduce desires the branches need cutting. Final liberation (*kaivalya* – absolute freedom) is attained when the roots of the tree are cut with discriminative wisdom and supreme dispassion. Then the mind (*citta*) and the afflictions (*kleśas*) are resolved back into its primal origin of *Prakṛiti* (the matter principle) and no longer exist as being separate. The mind and afflictions completely dissolve and cease to function as a mind.

> *These vṛtti states of mind produced by the afflictions are eliminated by meditation.*
> Patañjali Yoga Sūtra 2:11

In this *Sūtra* Patañjali tells us that it is the *kleśas* (afflictions) that produce the *vṛttis* or vortices of feeling, and that meditation (*dhyāna*) eliminates the more subtle *vṛttis* or the seeds of these afflictions.

Eliminating the *Kleśas* by *Kriya Yoga*

By themselves the *kleśas* cannot be weakened or eliminated without the methods of *Kriya Yoga*. So, Patañjali has given us three *Yoga* actions or methods that he terms as *Kriya Yoga*, which weakens the cycle of desires and attachments, habits and selfishness of the ego, and prepares the mind for *samādhi* (superconsciousness; absorption). The purpose for practising these three methods, known as *Kriya Yoga*, is to purify the mind by reducing gross manifestations of the *kleśas* (afflictions) with the aim of attaining *samādhi*. If we do not remove these *kleśas* of the mind it will not be possible to attain the superconscious state (*samādhi*).

These three practices of *Kriya Yoga* are particularly suited to those who are already established in spiritual disciplines and practices, but who have not completely mastered the practice of concentration. The three practices are integrally connected with each other and should be practised as such.

Tapaḥ svādhyāya īśvara-praṇidhānāni kriyāyogaḥ

Disciplining and purifying the senses, Self-study, and living in the presence of God constitute the practice of Yoga.
Patañjali Yoga Sūtra 2:1

The Sanskrit word *Tapaḥ* or *tapas* in this *sūtra* literally means 'to heat up' or 'to burn'. *Tapas* is purifying, it burns the impurities and desires in the mind.

Tapas does not mean mortification, suppression, nor repression. *Tapas* is an austerity in the sense of a discipline, and willingly accepting discomforts that limit the sense of ego. It is training the mind, body and senses to live the truth of who you are in reality. It is having control over your mind, body, senses, and *prāṇa* (life force).

Svādhyāya (Self-study) can be interpreted in two ways. One way is to study the sacred scriptures. The other way is introspection, observing your own mind to understand who you really are in essence. It is investigating the nature of the Self through inquiry to discover its origin, the source of consciousness. Study and observation purifies the intellect of ignorance, imbalances, and impurities.

Īśvara-praṇidhāna is constantly keeping the Divine Presence in the heart. It is an attitude of devotion, feeling the omnipresence of the Supreme Being. Through this practice one acquires steadiness of mind (*samāhita citta*) and ultimately the state of superconscious (*samādhi*).

Thus, the grosser aspects of the *kleśas* are eliminated by the three methods of *Kriya Yoga*. The subtle aspects are eliminated by meditation (*dhyāna*), but the residual impressions of the *saṁskāras* (subtle karmic impressions in the mind) are not completely extinguished until the mind and all its *saṁskāras* resolve back to its source, in the attainment of the final absorption in the Self (*Puruṣa*), in *Nirvikalpa samādhi*, which is synonymous with *asamprajñāta samādhi* – superconsciousness beyond all knowledge. The attainment of *asamprajñāta samādhi* burns the *kleśas* seeds so that they can never become active again. Thus, the primary affliction of ignorance (*avidyā*) is eliminated, from which the other afflictions originate.

The mind and the senses

We are all seeking happiness, and want freedom from sorrow and suffering. Most people generally seek it through external activities, in objects, people, or in anything that gives pleasure through sense enjoyment. The seeking is external, it is not ultimately fulfilling because the external objects of the senses have a changeable, temporary, and transient nature. When we try to find happiness through our desires and the senses, the mind becomes restless, unsteady, discontented and unfulfilled. There may be some temporary satisfaction and happiness when the desired object, person, or thing that we wanted is attained, but the mind does not remain happily content for long; happiness seems fleeting. All actions are motivated by desire and activated by *rajas guṇa* (activity, desire, passion). Without *rajas guṇa* or desire there is no movement of the senses, they remain still. When we control desire we restrain the senses.

Indulgence in the senses can only give us temporary gratification; it can never give us real happiness that is fulfilling and lasting. True happiness and freedom from sorrow and suffering is only possible when the desires and restlessness of the mind ceases. All desires are our longing for the divine Self within, and until we look within we will never find real happiness, for the external world is not the source of our spiritual fulfilment. The infinite, all-pervading universal Self is the ultimate source of happiness, peace, and joy.

An electricity power point can become weakened from loss of its voltage if there are too many electric connections that go beyond its limit. Likewise, the mind can become weak by connecting itself too much to the objects of the senses. But when all the connections are cut off, the power point meter immediately shows a rise in voltage. Similarly, one can perceive a rise in the voltage of the strength in the mind the moment the connections of the senses with their respective sense objects are cut off or disconnected. Patañjali says in his *Yoga Sūtras* (2:54) that *Pratyāhāra* is that state where the senses separate from the mind and appear to be one with the mind. They are no longer outside the mind, but have assumed the form of the mind itself.

The senses – a means for gathering experience

The five components of creation – ether, air, fire, water and earth – have given us our five senses: hearing, feeling, sight, taste and smell respectively.

The soul (the true Self) shines by its own light; it is the true source of intelligence which gives life to the body, mind and senses. Without the life force of the Self, the body, mind and senses cannot function at all.

Primarily (as young children prove) the senses are the first instruments to gather knowledge or perception from the external world. The reason I use the expression "to gather" is because awareness of sense perceptions arises only if the information delivered by the senses reaches the mind. Without mind there is no recorded perception and so the senses become useless as instruments.

When the mind receives the collected information from the senses it examines, analyses and discriminates what it has received and acts upon it. But what makes the senses go out and gather information? It is curiosity. So curiosity has to exist in the mind to determine it to send the senses out to gather information to satisfy that curiosity. But the more you try to satisfy your mind's curiosity, the more curiosity is generated, because each piece of information triggers more questions.

The mind has this inborn curiosity because it is searching for meaning. It wants to enlarge the whole informational picture until it makes sense. So curiosity, or the desire to find out and know things, is a search for meaning.

So why does the attempt of the mind and senses to find meaning in life fail so often? The senses are the means for gathering experience. Experience may be divided into pleasant and unpleasant, like and dislike. Each sensory experience leaves an impression (*saṁskāra*) on the mind. For example, when you first perceive an apple and touch it, smell it, and taste it, you have knowledge of an apple. An impression (*saṁskāra*) is immediately formed in the subconscious mind, and at any time this *saṁskāra* can generate a memory of the object – the apple and knowledge of the apple.

After accumulating a number of experiences that are alike, the mind forms an idea about them. So now the ego, the 'I-maker' which is born of ignorance (*avidyā*), intervenes, disregarding the truth or the reality that all these experiences come and go.

The ego says: "That was beautiful, I want to keep it. That is ugly, I want to avoid it." But neither of these is possible. If the beautiful thing we saw is not present, the mind which registered the experience as memory goes on wanting it; and what is even more unfortunate, the mind also remembers an unpleasant experience and goes on fearing it. It is not there, but you know it might come again. It also might not return, but the mind retains the impression of that momentary experience of pleasure or of displeasure, and out of this is born desire, like and dislike. When the momentary experience of pleasure born of sense contact is allowed to leave an impression on the mind, the mind becomes coloured by it, so that afterwards wherever you look, that thing continues to rotate in the mind – "I want that, I must have it," or "I want to have that, but I fear it may not happen."

Gradually the obstinate efforts to repeat pleasurable experiences and avoid unpleasant ones lead to an abandoning of the initial search – the search for meaning. Instead, one becomes addicted to sense pleasure and comfort, not understanding that pleasure is not in the objects but in the condition of the mind, and that happiness is not in the objects but within one's inner Self. Our lives become ruled by desire and attachment, and the need to defend what we think belongs to us.

What makes the senses function?

When you open your eyes, they see, and in that sight there is no love or hate. The sight also sees different colours. To some sights the eyes respond without blinking, and to some sights the eyes immediately want to close. These are natural, and the word natural means that they are inherent in all living beings. If the senses are to function naturally, they must function as decided by life and intelligence.

Does this experience, this impulse for expression, arise in life and intelligence, or is there an ego interference in it? In a simple way, did this impulse, or this action, or experience, arise from the intelligence or from the mind? The mind is the ego, the ego sense and the ego is the mind. When the question arises, a sudden change takes place within you – that is called *pratyāhāra*. That is, you are looking at something and you say, "Ah, that is beautiful, I love it," and immediately the question arises, "Is this from the mind or the intelligence?" When the question arises, the whole thing immediately turns back. Something that was externalising or flowing out immediately turns back. It is as simple as that.

Then that intelligence and that awareness itself is capable of ensuring that the experience or the expression is not ego motivated. The ego need not make any effort to shut out all these, so it is not as though when I see a beautiful face – "No, I don't want to see!"

That being an activity of the ego is useless to Yoga. If it is ego motivated rejection, it is still rejection, and if the ego finds it convenient, it will take it back some time later. It is the intelligence that raises this question, "Does it arise in the intelligence or is it ego motivated?" and that can eliminate all ego motivated expressions and experiences.

So the awareness is aware merely of the source of the action or the experience. This is *pratyāhāra* in a very different form of control. You will see, change is taking place in your behaviour and in your experience, but not because the ego decides that this is better than that, and not because the ego decides this is good and this is not good. A natural change takes place, and that change brings you into total alignment with this inner intelligence, and that is precisely how *pratyāhāra* is defined in the Yoga Sūtra: *"Citta svarūpānukāra"* (2:54).

That is, the senses function in total alignment with the inner intelligence which means there is no mind or ego interference. When that happens of course the ego reveals its nature. The awakened intelligence sees the countless ways in which the ego tries to step in and pollute actions and experiences.

Dulling of the senses

The other intervening phenomenon is a dulling of the senses due to overindulgence and repetition. The drug addict starts with marijuana and goes on to take stronger and more dangerous drugs like cocaine and heroin. The smoker smokes more cigarettes. The drinker drinks more, and ends up becoming an alcoholic. The relationship that becomes more and more sexual, based on physical self-gratification without love, soon becomes dull and repetitive, and so one or both partners continually look for more stimulating and exciting forms of sex with other partners, whom become mere objects of stimulation. Whether it is drugs, alcohol, sex, smoking, coffee or sugar, indulgence in any pleasure dulls the sensitivity of the senses and the nervous system. In the end it will either bore you or enslave you, and in that there is no freedom, beauty, or joy. The initial stimulus is no longer strong enough to cause pleasure. The initial sharpness and awareness of the sense-experience wears off, and the senses need a stronger one in order for the ego to have the kind of pleasure it expects.

The ego's relation to experience

The way the ego relates to experience is also wrong, in that it wants to possess the objects of attachment. The ego is frustrated by the fleetingness of pleasure and wants to externalise it through possession. In fact, possession is a delusion. We do not even own what we eat. We just recycle energies, and not even that process is a conscious one. Possessiveness 'freezes' the relationship with the object or person.

Instead of using our senses to discover the meaning at the interface of any process of relating, we want to 'have' this or that experience out of it. What gets lost again is the meaning, the teaching that we receive. We unwittingly refer to the ego rather than to the real *Self.*

False identification with the object of the senses

> *Egoism* (*asmitā* – I-am-ness, sense of individuality) *is the false identification of the Seer* (*puruṣa*, Self) *with the instrument of cognition* (*buddhi*, intellect or mind).
> Patañjali Yoga Sūtra 2:6

The body, mind, and senses are the non-Self (unconscious principle) that are evolutes of *Prakṛiti* (material nature). The Self (*puruṣa*) is the eternal conscious principle.

Although the Self (*puruṣa* – the subjective power of consciousness) and the intellect-mind (*buddhi* – the instrument of cognition) are completely different, when the mind is covered by ignorance (*avidyā*) they appear as if they were the same. The reflection of the Self on the intellect-mind produces the separate ego sense of 'I'. Due to ignorance (*avidyā*) the intellect-mind acts as if it is the Self. This delusive affliction is known as *asmitā kleśa* (affliction of ego).

It is not the object that binds or enslaves you. It is the false identification of the thought with the object that causes desire, possessiveness, attachment, and fear. It is the identification and labelling of things as 'desirable' and 'undesirable' by the ego that causes all the problems. The mind labels a sensation or experience desirable, which automatically makes its opposite or absence undesirable – pleasure creates pain. The sensation becomes a feeling at the point when thought arises to label the sensations. The labelling creates division between the thought and the experience. In pure experiencing there is no labelling. In the state of pure awareness, the mind is undivided and steady. If the mind seeks the experience of something other than the inner joy and inner peace of the Self, the awareness of its own nature is lost or hidden.

When the futility of desire and the pursuit of sensory objects are seen, the mind is left with the feeling that something is lacking or missing. It is forgetfulness of our true essential nature – the blissful Self within. That which is missing is the inner joy and inner peace of Self-fulfilment. We have lost the memory and awareness of our original blissful state. Through misidentification with the ego-self we try to find happiness and fulfilment with the fleeting joys of sensory pleasures. The reason we search with continual determination for true happiness and joy is that we have the memory of our true nature. The individual soul is inwardly conscious of losing its blissful contact with the Supreme Consciousness, the source of all joy, peace, and love, the one and only Reality of our being, and can never remain satisfied with the limited pleasures of the senses. Eventually, every soul must awaken to their true divine nature and return to Oneness.

Mastery of the senses

Lord Krishna teaches us in in the *Bhāgavad Gīta* that if the senses are not controlled, the mind will be distracted and captivated by attachment to sensory experiences, leading to forgetfulness of one's true essential nature – the Self:

Just as a tortoise draws in its limbs within its shell, the wise yogi, fixed in higher consciousness, disconnects the senses from their objects of perception at will, resulting in steadiness of mind.

Those who deprive the senses from experiencing their objects experience that they still crave for them. These sense cravings only come to an end when one attains a higher knowledge and realises the Self.

Having brought the senses under control one should be joined in yoga with the mind ever established in Me. The wisdom of one who has mastered the senses becomes steadfast and unwavering.

The senses become attached to an object when it is continually thought of. As a result of such involvement, the desire to enjoy the object arises. When such a desire is unfulfilled or obstructed, anger arises.

Anger clouds discrimination and one falls easily into illusion, losing the memory of one's own true Self. From loss of memory one loses the faculty of discrimination and eventually from the confusion of intelligence misses the goal of human life – Self-realisation.

However, those who can supervise the involvement between the senses and sense objects by exercising self-control, and who become free from craving and false repression attain inner calmness and peace.

In that inner calmness and inner joy comes the end of all sorrows. For the intelligence of the calm-minded soon becomes firmly established in the Self.

For one whose mind and senses are unsteady, there is no knowledge of the Self. When the mind is restless it cannot concentrate or meditate; it has no peace. Without inner peace, how can there be joy?

Just as a boat on the sea is carried away by the wind in a storm, so can a person's intelligence and understanding be carried away by the force of sense desire.

Therefore, one whose senses are completely mastered becomes firmly established in wisdom of the Self.

Just as the vast ocean remains calm and unperturbed, even though many rivers flow into it from all sides, so a person should remain undivided by the continued arising of sense desires. One who is controlled by desire cannot attain true peace.

True inner peace arises when all sense desires are transcended and orientated to higher levels of consciousness; and when one acts free from identification with the false ego and the illusion of the sense of 'I' and 'mine'.

Bhāgavad Gīta 2:58–71

The practice of *Pratyāhāra*

The difference between a Master of *Yoga* and an ordinary worldly person is that the yogi experiences true joy, inner peace, and contentment by inwardly reversing the searchlight of perception from the senses to the divine source within, *consciously at will*. The worldly person, whose ego-mind identifies with and is attached to the senses, becomes disunited from the inner source of joy and peace – the Self. Instead, the worldly person suffers restlessly with anger, fear and loss of inner peace and joy.

The worldly person can only disconnect the mind from the senses in the *subconscious* state of ordinary sleep; the life force that connects the mind with the senses reverts back to the Self-conscious force of the soul. In this state of sleep there is no consciousness of 'I'. There is no desire to experience; there is no ego-sense. In sleep you are not aware that 'I am'; otherwise you are awake! What remains is pure experiencing – there is no contact with the objects of the senses, and since there is no contact, the mind is not divided. That is why you do not experience pain or suffering at all during sleep.

In the dream state during sleep, the senses of perception are still and absorbed in the mind. It is only the mind that is actively operating during a dream; it becomes both the subject and the object. During the wakeful state objects exist independently of the mind. Whether you are asleep or awake the objects are always there. However, in dreams the objects exist only as long as there is the mind to create them and for as long as the dream lasts. When you awake from your sleep all the dream objects disappear.

In sleep there is no time, no space, no objects other than you. You have gone to sleep, your mind and senses have withdrawn inward. The outer world of objects and people vanishes, but an inner world of images arises from within you. A world that seems real as a dream while you sleep, but unreal when you awaken from that dream.

That same world that projects your dream experiences in sleep can become very active when you sit for meditation and try to concentrate your mind by disconnecting it from the outer world (*Prakṛiti*) experience. The inner world or inner *Prakṛiti* arises in the form of countless *saṁskāras*, *vāsanās* and memories that are submerged and latent in the *citta* (field of consciousness). Thoughts and feelings spontaneously arise in the mind and distract you as you try to concentrate. As a distracting thought arises you become associated with that thought and the thought current begins to flow in numerous directions. And losing your concentration and Self-awareness, you get swept away in that distracting thought current.

The reason why these distracting thoughts arise when you sit to concentrate for meditation is because when you are engaged in other daily activities and experiences on the outer plane, or engaged in some process that requires your attention, your mind is drawn outward and gets engaged in that process. So the inner process of *saṁskāras*, *vāsanās*, and memories taking the form of *vṛttis*, mental modifications, becomes restricted. Whereas when you are sitting for meditation with your mind and attention withdrawn from the outer world, a vacuum is created in the mind, which invites from deep within your subconscious the submerged and latent *saṁskāras*, *vāsanās*, memories, and seeds of suppressed and unfulfilled desires, which are stimulated by *rāga-dveṣa* (attraction and aversion).

Training the mind to be clear, calm and one-pointed

Abhyāsa (practice) and *Vairāgya* (non-attachment)

> *The stilling of the vṛtti states of mind is achieved by (persistent) practice and non-attachment.*
> Patañjali Yoga Sūtra 1:12

Due to restlessness the mind is continually moving toward outer objects and becoming dissipated. When your mind becomes scattered, it becomes gross and limited in its function and power, and you lose awareness of your true inner spiritual nature. It is only when your mind flows inward and is absolutely calm and quiet and unified in a subtle state that your own inner spiritual God-Self is revealed to you. Then you perceive that everything is a manifestation of the Divine Reality.

The practice of *Kriya Yoga* weakens the restlessness of the mind with all its desires and attachments, and prepares the mind for two practices that when practised together help to acquire a clear, calm and one-pointed mind. *Abhyāsa* strengthens renunciation, and the detachment of *abhyāsa* deepens meditation.

Abhyāsa – regular and persistent practice of one-pointed meditation to redirect the mind toward discriminative wisdom. For practice to be firmly established, it has to be practised with earnest dedication over a long and uninterrupted period of time.

Vairāgya – non-attachment or dispassion. Cultivating a mind free from the 'colouring' of deep latent subtle karmic impressions (*vāsanās*) that bring about worldly desires, that include *vṛttis* such as anger, lust, greed, attachment, likes and dislikes, and develop into bad habits.

By practising *abhyāsa* and *vairāgya* you will be able to have control over your body-mind, senses, speech, and actions. With this mastery over your mind you are then able to eliminate all unwanted habits and direct your energy into creating new spiritual habits that will bring you deep inner peace, contentment, true happiness and joy.

The mind is, by nature, restless (*chanchala*) and unsteady (*a-sthira*). It can neither constantly think of one object nor consistently think of different objects. In the *Bhāgavad Gīta* (6:24–28) Lord Krishna also instructs us how the restless and unsteady mind can be controlled. The following verses 24 to 35 give a description of spiritual practice (*sādhanā*) to inspire the aspirant. In the two significant verses 24 and 25, the subtle art of meditation has been explained. It instructs us that it is not sufficient that all desires are renounced, but that each desire that arises must be *totally* and fully eradicated; even the desire for perfection in Yoga. As you gradually conquer your habits, and desires for pleasure and sense-gratification, your mind becomes stronger, giving you the capacity to control your senses by withdrawing the mind inward in meditation, away from the world of sense-objects. You accomplish this slowly and patiently. After withdrawing the senses, the mind's flow of thought is directed in a steady concentrated flow toward the indwelling Self, the Divine Presence within (that is immanent in everything). The mind is very subtle and can move quickly. If the mind wanders back to the objects of the senses, you slowly and patiently bring it back from its wanderings. With firm determination, the mind becomes one-pointed in the steady contemplation of the inner Self. In this inward silence you reach that state of deep inner calmness, inner peace, and with conscious unbroken awareness, undisturbed by any agitations, thoughts or feelings, you abide in your true essential and blissful infinite nature *as* the Self. With the mind's attention turned inward toward the Self it *directly* experiences the nature of the Self as pure Consciousness. *"That pure Consciousness am I."* It is only when the mind is free from all desires, likes and dislikes, and is detached from the sense objects, that it can abide in the Self.

> *Abandoning entirely without exception all desires arising from self-intention, and completely restraining all the senses by determined intelligence.*
> Bhāgavad Gīta 6:24

> *One should through gradual practice attain inner calmness; and having established the mind in the Self, relinquish all other thoughts.*
> Bhāgavad Gīta 6:25

> *Whenever the restless and unsteady mind wanders away, from that, withdraw it and redirect it back to be under control of the Self alone.*
> Bhāgavad Gīta 6:26

> *For the Yogi, whose mind is perfectly calm, whose passion is quieted, who is freed from all impurity, attains supreme bliss in oneness with the supreme Self.*
> Bhāgavad Gīta 6:27

> *Thus, uniting the Self in Yoga, the Yogi, free of all imperfections, easily attains the infinite blissful union in the Divine.*
> Bhāgavad Gīta 6:28

> *Without doubt, the mind is unsteady, and difficult to control.*

> *However, it can be controlled by practice (abhyāsa) and dispassion (vairāgya).*
> Bhāgavad Gīta 6:35

It teaches us that the restless and turbulent mind can be controlled by continuous practice (*abhyāsa*) and that the natural flow of the mind toward outer objects of sense pleasure can be removed by non-attachment and dispassion (*vairāgya*).

> *Meditate daily, with earnestness and devotion.*
> *Love God without ceasing.*
> Paramhansa Yogananda

When the mind becomes free from distractions caused by sense objects and the mind is grounded in one-pointed concentration, then the mind is able to flow inward and become stable through the regular practice of meditation. Without regular practice (*abhyāsa*) you will not be able to attain a clear, calm, and one-pointed mind, and you will not make spiritual progress.

Developing stability of mind

Patañjali, in his *Yoga Sūtras* 1:35–39, gives several methods of bringing steadiness and stability to the mind by using different objects of meditation.

> *Or concentration on the subtle sense perceptions also firmly establishes the steadiness of the mind.*
> Yoga Sūtra 1:35

This *sūtra* is referring to the spontaneous manifestation of subtle sense perception. It is in the subtle realm of the senses (*tanmātra*) in the astral body that the mind is captivated, destroying doubt, and making the mind become one-pointed. In meditation we can concentrate on the higher subtle sense of listening to the inner sounds of the *chakras* and to *Aum*. In deep meditation with the eyes closed concentrating at the midpoint between the eyebrows (spiritual eye) we can see the inner light. Other subtle manifestations can be experienced by concentration on the subtle sense perceptions such as fragrance, taste and touch, leading to the subtle nature of the object. Through the direct experience of deep concentration, inner knowledge and dispassion for the lower stages of concentration is attained.

> *Or (the mind becomes calm and steady) by concentrating on the supreme, ever-blissful light within, that is beyond sorrow.*
> Yoga Sūtra 1:36

This *sūtra* is a continuation of the preceding *sūtra* in the sense that it causes steadiness and calmness of the mind. The previous *sūtra* relates to concentration on the subtle senses and subtle elements (*tanmātra*). This *sūtra* (1:36) is referring to the internal objects as the manifestation of the light of *sattva*. Only the awareness of 'I-am' is experienced (*asmitā mātra jyotishmatī*).

This subject-focused meditation is different from the concentration on the subtle sense perceptions, which have an external object such as fragrance or taste, since the object is the *puruṣa* (Self, soul) itself. Sorrow (*viśokā*) is an indicator of distracted attention; when our calm attention is one-pointed concentration on the inner light (the luminous Self within), which is free from *rajas* and *tamas*, steadiness and calmness of mind is attained. We become freed from all mental distractions, and sorrow.

> *Or (the mind becomes calm and steady) by attunement with the consciousness of an enlightened being who has transcended desire and attachment to sense-objects.*
> Yoga Sūtra 1:37

To gain inner stability of the mind you can also meditate on an enlightened being who is perfectly established in the principle of non-attachment (*vairagya*). Such a pure enlightened being or true guru beyond ego-consciousness is free from conditioning, desires, attachments, likes and dislikes. By attuning your will to the guru's will you can be guided by his or her wisdom to find perfect freedom in God. The guru and his teachings are a channel for the Divine Will, or Supreme Being, to reach the Truth-seeking soul. When you are in attunement with the guru, you connect your life with Supreme Consciousness. The guru will guide you and help you to remain steadfast in the spiritual principles that you need to succeed on the spiritual path.

By remaining loyal and attuned to the wise, enlightened guru your mind will develop dispassion for the objects of the senses. The mind will become steady, and when you meditate you will be able to enter deep within the calmness of your true inner Self.

Attune yourself to the enlightened guru by keeping him ever in your heart. Be one with him in principle. Visualise your guru or take a picture of him, and sitting still with no other thoughts, concentrate on his eyes or his spiritual eye. Meditate on his omnipresence, the spiritual consciousness beyond his physical form. Feel that you are seated in his divine presence, that he is meditating with you. Pray to him: "Divine Master, bless me, guide me, and protect me, show me the true path to Self-realisation." Become absorbed in that one prayerful thought, then in the silence and inner communion, wait for an answer by listening and feeling his presence in your own heart. You will be guided by soul-intuition from within and pointed in the right direction.

My guru, Paramhansa Yogananda, said that without a guru it is very difficult to find God. It requires 25% of devoted practice of meditation; 25% blessings of the guru; and 50% grace of God. But if you remain steady in your efforts to the end, God will appear before you.

Or (the mind becomes calm and steady) by concentration on the insightful wisdom (prājñā) gained in dream or deep sleep states.
Yoga Sūtra 1:38

In sleep you forget the world; even the 'I-am-the-body' awareness does not exist. The 'I' experience does not exist in sleep. When you are asleep, you are not consciously aware that you are sleeping; you do not say, "I sleep."

During the dream state (*svapna*) the experiencer of the dream is only conscious of internal objects. The senses are quiet and absorbed in the mind. The consciousness of the individual is withdrawn from the physical senses and becomes identified with the subtle body, the waking state temporarily disappears and the consciousness enters the dream state. In this dream state, the individual consciousness is restricted to the *antaḥkaraṇa*, the fourfold inner instrument, consisting of the *manas* (deliberation), *buddhi* (determination), *ahaṁkāra* (egoism or I-ness) and *citta* (recollection). The dream state and images are projected inwardly upon the mental screen from impressions seen during the waking state. When these impressions and the external objects are modified and left in the mind the individual experiences dreams.

In the dreamless deep sleep state (*sushupti*) there is an absence of mental activity; there is no thinking, feeling, nor sensory perception. The individual is not conscious or aware of anything. But this is not negative, or a state of non-existence, for on waking we are happy and conscious of having slept a sound and restful sleep. We feel we existed even during sleep. In comparison to the waking and dreaming states of mental activity, whose characteristic is the presence of a knower and a known, or a thinker and a thought, in dreamless sleep the principle of consciousness remains and exits without its seeming to assume the duality of a conscious subject and object. Consciousness is continuous.

In deep dreamless sleep (*nidra*; *sushupti*), the mental functions cease altogether, there is no thinker to think thoughts, there is no awareness of thoughts or 'I', there is no ego and no world. The Self recedes even from the mind. Both the five organs of perception, and the mind, remain hidden and latent, suspended in a state of ignorance (*ajñāna*), within the blissful sheath of the causal body.

During dreamless sleep the soul is united with consciousness, the nature of absolute bliss. But this is not the transcendental state or the fourth, known as *turīya*, in which the consciousness merges into the *ātmān* (Self). This union is only apparent, it is only a reflection; it is not the true union or superconsciousness that follows the knowledge and realisation of the Self. The sleeping individual returns to the consciousness of the waking state and returns to his conditioned personality, with the same habits, desires and attachments. The individual self remembers that it had a happy and sound sleep. This recollection results from experience therefore there must be experience in the deep dreamless sleep (*nidra*; *sushupti*).

The recollection of the pleasant and joyful feeling from deep dreamless sleep brings an experience of inner calmness and peace, which can be used as an object of meditation in the wakeful state (*jagrat*).

In the dream state (*svapna*) one can have a spiritual dream or a superconscious dream in which a revered guru, saint or deity appears. Awakening from such a spiritual dream brings peace and joy to the mind and heart. By recollecting and remembering the spiritual dream one can become absorbed in that vision, then the mind becomes calm and steady in meditation. Insights gained in the *svapna* and *nidra* states can calm and steady the mind.

In 1982, when I first met swami Kriyananda (a direct disciple of Paramhansa Yogananda) in London, I had a superconscious dream in which Paramhansa Yogananda (1893–1952) appeared personally to me. The purpose of him appearing in the spiritual dream to me was to remove any doubt that he was my guru. Yogananda stood before me and in his calm but authoritative voice said:

> *I am your guru, Paramhansa Yogananda. You no longer need to search for a guru, I am your guru and Kriya Yoga is the path you will now follow.*

In the morning when I awoke from the dream, I felt a great sense of joy and happiness and peace within. The memory of my dream was so vivid and clear in my mind, it felt very real and meaningful. I was so inspired that Yogananda had appeared to me, that my mind remained in a joyful, calm and steady state throughout the whole day. Now whenever I remember that dream experience, my mind turns inward and becomes stabilised in the *sattvic* state of calmness, peace, and joy, and devotion.

> *Or by meditating on any chosen object that is spiritually elevating, one attains steadiness of mind.*
> Yoga Sūtra 1:39

In this *sūtra*, *Patañjali* concludes this subject of the six methods for stilling the mind by saying that we may choose any object of meditation according to our preference. In other words, any method or object that is agreeable to the mind, that brings steadiness and calmness, and one-pointedness to the mind can be used for meditation.

According to our temperaments and particular spiritual tradition that we follow, we may have different inclinations toward a particular object or method of meditation. For example, one who has an emotional temperament may find a natural preference for the method given in Sūtra 1:37. This may be the image of Krishna or Jesus Christ, or a revered guru such as Paramhansa Yogananda.

Twenty qualities of a spiritually awakened mind

In the *Bhāgavad Gīta*, chapter 13, verses 7–12, Lord Krishna enumerates twenty qualities of the mind, which he declares to be *jñana* – true spiritual knowledge, or wisdom to be known. The twenty qualities include mental and emotional attributes, moral attitudes and ethical principles. These twenty qualities of gaining knowledge of the Infinite Self will help you to attain a quiet mind to abide in the inner Self.

Amānitvam adambhitvam ahiṁsā kṣāntirārjavam
ācāryopāsanaṁ śaucaṁ sthairyam ātmavinigrahaḥ (13:7)

1. Humility (*Amānitvam*)
Absence of self-pride, being free from the sense of self-importance. Not seeking recognition. The rains of God's grace (the highest gift from the Divine) cannot gather on the mountain peaks of pride, but flow easily into the valleys of humility.

2. Unpretentiousness (*Adāmbhitvam*)
This implies the same principle of integrity or being true to oneself. It is not attempting to impress others with an appearance of greater importance, talent, or culture than is actually possessed.

3. Harmlessness (*Ahiṁsā*)
Non-harming, not causing pain or suffering to any living beings. Your intentions, thoughts, feelings and actions should be non-harming.

4. Acceptance (*Kṣāntiḥ*)
Forbearance and tolerance in the face of difficult circumstances and insults. Forgiveness and patience.

5. Straightforwardness (*Ārjavam*)
Straightforwardness and uprightness, being honest and frank. Your thoughts, words and deeds should be in harmonious agreement, with the intent on right behaviour and right conduct.

6. Service to the guru (*Ācāryopāsanaṁ*)

Real service to the authentic guru who is committed to serving unconditionally is to seek an attunement mentally and spiritually with the guru's mind and heart. The student has one responsibility, and that is to spiritually open and grow. The purpose of a guru is to spiritually awaken you, to transform your consciousness, to free you from your limited understanding, and to guide you toward establishing direct contact with the God within you.

To truly serve the guru you have get beyond your own desires and limitations, and resistance to giving, and transform yourself into a conscious instrument of God. True service happens from the heart not the mind; it is a natural expression of the love, devotion, and gratitude that you feel from an open heart, that allows Grace to emerge from within you. This gives you the willingness and capacity to serve unconditionally.

7. Inner and outer purity (*Śaucaṁ*)

Outer cleanliness is keeping your body clean (hygiene), and your home or work environment clean and tidy. Internal cleanliness is purity of the mind – purity of thoughts, emotions, intentions and motives, and right attitude. An impure mind is tainted by negative emotions associated to likes and dislikes: selfishness, anger, hatred, resentment, jealousy, envy, fear, guilt, pride, possessiveness. To overcome such negative emotions, use your willpower to think of positive thoughts opposite to the negative thoughts.

The best way to purify the mind is to think and live in the Truth, from that divine Self which you are. Your sincerity and earnestness to realise the ultimate Truth will purify your mind.

8. Steadfastness (*Sthairyam*)

Steadfastness or constancy on the path of righteousness by one who has accepted it. You should have a consistency of purpose and concentration of all efforts toward achieving your spiritual goal.

9. Mastery over the mind (*Ātmavinigrahaḥ*)
True control or mastery of the mind means to keep the mind absorbed in the Self (*ātmā*) within and not allowing it to run wild with desires, wrong attitudes, wrong or negative thinking. One should understand that any pleasure received by the senses (*indriyas*) through worldly material attachments is short-lived.

Indriyārtheṣu vairāgyam anahaṁkāra eva ca
janmamṛtyujarāvyādhiduḥkhadoṣānudarśanam (13:8)

10. Dispassion toward objects of the senses
(*Indriyārtheṣu vairāgyam*)
You can live with the objects of the world, but be careful not to become preoccupied with them, for this leads to attachment and to sorrow. *Vairāgya* means dispassion. Through dispassion there is an awakening of spiritual awareness; the flow of the mind is directed away from the distractions of objects of desire. Dispassion is realising that the end result of indulgence in worldly desires is suffering (*duḥkha*).

11. Absence of egotism (*Anahaṁkāra eva ca*)
Relinquish false ego, and identification of the body as the Self. The individual sense of 'I' is present when you *falsely identify* yourself (the 'I') with your body, mind, ego, thoughts, feelings and emotions. In its identification and attachment to the world of matter, the ego (*ahaṁkāra*), the 'perceiver' and 'enjoyer' of the material world, likes and dislikes, loves and hates, enjoys and suffers.

Absence of egotism also means not proclaiming your own greatness for any achievement (absence of self-pride), for there may be other factors responsible for an achievement that is not solely yours.

To relinquish your identification with the ego, direct your thought to your real nature, Self or Consciousness, which is beyond the reach of the ego. When you are calmly centred in the changeless Self, the limitations of thought disappear. Affirm: *"I am Consciousness"*, *"I am pure Consciousness"*; it is beyond the limitations of the ego and it will draw you inward, to ultimately merge in the 'I' or 'Consciousness'.

Or you can simply contemplate: *"I am."* These two words give your mind nothing objective to attach to. All intruding thoughts are driven away, so that you are established in pure Consciousness and Joy – the intrinsic qualities of the 'I' that transcends the body, senses and mind.

12. Reflect on the limitations of birth, death, old age, disease and pain (*Janma-mṛtyu-jarā-vyādhi-duḥkha-doṣānu-darśanam*)

All living beings are subject to birth, disease, old age, and death. We all experience the detrimental effect of sorrow, caused by pain (*duḥkha*), birth (*janma*), disease (*vyādhi*), old age (*jarā*), and death (*mṛtyu*) in our material existence. What is born will also die. All that lives in the material world is subject to limitation. Life is temporary and time is precious, so it should not be wasted. Make good use of your time. Be grateful for the body that you have and for the gift of physical life that was provided to you. Accomplish all of your meaningful purposes during your present incarnation, including the ultimate purpose for your sojourn in this world – to be spiritually liberated.

Asaktiranabhiṣvaṅgaḥ putradāragṛhādiṣu
ṇityaṁ ca samacittatvam iṣṭāniṣṭopapattiṣu (13:9)

13. Non-attachment (*Asaktiḥ*)

The absence of the attitude of ownership. Everything you are in possession of is temporary and impermanent, including your own body. You, the immortal Self, are the indweller of your body, and have been entrusted to care for it and maintain it. When you can see your relationship to things and sense objects objectively, dispassionately – that they cannot give you lasting happiness or security – you will not become attached to them. Attachment is about need and the fear of losing. Attachment constrains and limits you and those people around you; it can only bring sorrow and pain. So cultivate an attitude that you do not own anything, and that you only possess them temporarily. In order to be free, discover within you that place that is unconditionally fulfilled that does not need anything. Non-attachment is not that you should not own anything, but that nothing should own you.

14. Non-identification of the ego with one's own children, wife and home, and so on (*Anabhiṣvanga*)

Our worldly attachments are finite and subject to change; they are non-permanent. Love, care and affection toward one's family is natural, but when it becomes excessive and possessive to such an extent, it causes attachment, leading in the end to sorrow and suffering (*duḥkha*). When there is an intense form of attachment toward family relations, property or objects, we mistakenly equate happiness with them. True happiness is being one with it. To know true happiness, never objectify it or separate it from you. Spiritually, you *are* happiness; it is your divine nature. Nothing needs to be added to you for you to experience, *"I am happiness."* You can never be happy; you can only *be* happiness. Your essential nature is *Sat-Cit-Ānanda* (ever-existent, ever-conscious, ever-new Joy).

With dispassion, and even-mindedness there is freedom from clinging to and intensely involved attachment to family relations, home and property. The attitude referred to here does *not* mean indifference – a lack of concern, care or sympathy – toward family relations, but an attitude of caring without intense involved attachment.

15. Constant even-mindedness toward desired and undesired circumstances (*Nityaṁ samacittatvam iṣṭā-aniṣṭa-upapattiṣu*)

This is maintaining equanimity (*samacittatvam*), mental calmness in all situations – in difficult situations, in success and in failure. It is accepting both the good and the bad with equanimity.

Mayi cānanyayogena bhaktiravyabhicāriṇi
viviktadeśasevitvam aratirjanasaṁsadi (13:10)

16. Unswerving devotion and identity with Me (the Self) with single-minded Yoga (*Mayi cānanya-yogena bhaktiḥ avyabhicāriṇi*)
Do not stray from the spiritual path that joins you with the Divine Reality, the Supreme Consciousness; keep your sight constantly on the indwelling Self. In Yoga, concentration (*dhāraṇā*) is holding and focusing the mind on that higher aspect of consciousness that is sometimes called the Supreme Self, which unsurpassed is the source of all knowledge. It is the ultimate Consciousness beyond the mind. It is eternal, unchangeable, and to experience it is to abide in one's own essential nature. Otherwise one identifies with the mind's activities. If your devotion wavers, then your practice of concentration becomes unsteady. There has to be undivided *attention* and *enthusiasm* to accomplish concentration, otherwise the mind will restlessly wander away into futile daydreaming and imaginations. Unswerving devotion is maintaining a continuous consciousness and presence of the Divine on all occasions.

17. Preference and fondness for a secluded place
(*Viviktadeśasevitvam*)
An integrated life of steady contemplation and meditation on a firm ideal is impossible, unless you practise in a conducive environment.

Vivikta means separate or solitary, and *sevitva* is to inhabit or resort to. *Deśa* means 'place'. This is the person who appreciates and enjoys being in solitude in a peaceful, quiet secluded place, with nothing obtruding into or disturbing his/her peace. The person is happy and content in following an enchanting and all-absorbing spiritual ideal, in quiet contemplation or meditation in a secluded place away from the noisy crowd. It is not an escape from oneself.

We only escape when we feel unhappy and incomplete, and are unable to face ourselves.

18. Disinclination for worldly society (*Aratiḥ janasaṁsadi*)
Craving and seeking the social company of others can be a form of escape from yourself. The spiritually minded person or meditator is not afraid of people, and he/she does not run after them either. He/she can be happy and content by themselves. This should not be misunderstood as escapism or aversion to society.

Adhyātmajñananityatvaṁ tattvajñānārthadarsanam
etajjñānam iti proktam ajñānaṁ yadato'nyathā (13:11)

19. Constancy in the pursuit of Self-realisation
(*Adhyātma-jñana-nityatvaṁ*)
Adhyātma means being centred on *ātmān* (the indwelling Self); *jñana* means knowledge, and *nityatva* means constancy, steadiness. *Adhyātma-jñana* means spiritual knowledge related to the Self (*ātmā*); Self-realisation.

Constantly (*nityam*) and steadily, be interested in spiritual knowledge, Self-realisation, and the immortal Self within. Always keep in mind your spiritual goal of liberation by reflecting, contemplating, meditating, and engaging your total being in understanding the purpose and aim of your life.

20. Aspiration toward Self-knowledge
(*Tattva-jñānārtha-darśanam*)
Darśanam means 'keeping in sight', *tattva-jñana* means 'of knowledge of the Truth'.

Seek the knowledge of the truth of yourself. Remember constantly your ultimate goal in life: to seek the pure knowledge of the Self, and aspire to it with enthusiasm, willingness, energy and joy. Realisation of the Self and liberation (*mokṣa*) from all imperfections and limitations is the spiritual goal. Seek to transcend your own duality and sense of separation from your Divine Source. Focusing on the highest level of consciousness is a completely conscious choice you must make moment by moment, day by day. Choose to live in the experience of inner freedom, peace, joy, and unconditional love.

All these qualities constitute wisdom. Ignorance, absence of knowledge, is the contrary of the above twenty qualities (*ajñānaṁ yadatoṁse qua*). Egotism, pride, conceit, hatred, thoughts of harming, hurting or cheating others, and the desire for sense-gratification and worldly enjoyments, are characteristic qualities of the ignorant, who are not aware of the true Self within. Even-mindedness, integrity, compassion, kindness, forgiveness, love, tolerance, patience, giving service to one's teachers and guru, and maintaining a steady practice of meditation and spirituality are the qualities and virtues of the spiritually wise.

In order to change your experience of life, you must change your consciousness. To progress and be successful spiritually in realising the Truth, and to expand your consciousness, the above twenty qualities or principles should be constantly practised with a steadfast devotion.

When you become firmly established in the knowledge that you are not this mind-body or ego-personality, and that only desire and habit separate you from Self-awareness, you will know that the eternal divine transcendent Self resides within you, *as* you. In that divine consciousness you abide in oneness with Spirit.

Part Two

The Different States of Consciousness

Death

The physical body is subject to change, death and decay because it is born in time, is extended in space, and subject to the law of causation. That change is inherent in every fleeting moment and there can be no renewal without death. This law applies to the entire phenomenal universe, which also exists within time, space and causation, and is constantly changing. The law of causation is a universal law that keeps the inner harmony and the logical order of the universe – the sun shines, the rivers flow, the wind blows, the rain falls, trees blossom and bear fruit, one season follows another, night follows day – all phenomena of Nature work in harmony and are governed by the one universal law of causation, which is also known as the law of *karma* – the eternal law of cause and effect.

At the time of physical death (which is not the end or annihilation of an individual being) the soul or the Self, which animates the body, withdraws from the physical form clothed in the astral and causal bodies. The lifeline which transmits life-energy (*prāṇa*) to the physical and mental sheaths becomes severed; the consciousness frees itself from the limitations of the physical and becomes associated with the subtle body. The *Ātmān* (true Self) is within and outside the body, and separate from it. The *Ātmān* is immortal, eternal, and is our permanent abode. Unlike the physical body *Ātmān*, the real Self within is not subject to birth and death. Even after the destruction of the body we shall continue to exist. Death is only the habit of the body, not of the soul.

After death, the soul continues to exist in the vehicle of the astral body (mind, intellect, ego, subtle sense organs, and the five vital airs). This carries with it *saṁskāras* (past impressions) or *karma* of all one's actions, thoughts, desires, merits, demerits, good and evil tendencies, and capacities. These are factors that determine the individual soul's journey beyond. Just as a person's inner attitudes and thoughts determine their life's course before death, so do they after their death.

Three different planes of consciousness

The embodied self, the experiencer within, daily experiences three different states of consciousness – **waking** (*jagrat*), **dream** (*svapna*), and **dreamless deep sleep** (*sushupti*). These three states are variable but the self who is experiencing them remains constant; it continues unmodified throughout the three states, from birth to death and beyond. The person experiencing says, "I wake," "I dream," "I sleep." It is the same "I" or experiencer in all three states of consciousness but does not belong to any of them.

The waking state

During the waking state the individual self, associated with the five sense organs, five motor organs, the five vital forces, and the mind connect with the various external objects by means of the modifications of the mind, which constitute the limiting adjuncts of the soul, and apprehends these external objects and identifies itself with the physical body. The individual is aware of the external objects and also of the conscious mental states, but not aware of the hidden subconscious propensities.

The waking state, like the dream state, is a projection of *maya* (cosmic illusion). As the reality experienced by the dreamer disappears on awakening, so too does the reality of the waking state disappear during the dream state. The waking state of consciousness does not exist in dream or sleep. It is therefore illusory. Reality always exists in all conditions or states.

The dream state

During the dream state the experiencer of the dream is only conscious of internal objects. The senses are quiet and absorbed in the mind. The consciousness of the individual is withdrawn from the physical senses and becomes identified with the subtle body, the waking state temporarily disappears and the consciousness enters the dream state. In this dream state, the individual consciousness is restricted to the *antaḥkaraṇa*, the fourfold inner instrument, consisting of the *manas* (deliberation), *buddhi* (determination), *ahaṁkāra* (egoism or I-ness) and *citta* (recollection). The dream state and images are projected inwardly upon the mental screen from impressions seen during the waking state. When these impressions and the external objects are modified and left in the mind the individual experiences dreams.

The difference between the waking state and the dream state

In the waking state, the mind depends on outward impressions, while in the dream state it creates and enjoys its own impressions. In dreams the objects exist only as long as there is the mind to dream them, and as long as the dream lasts. As soon as the mind returns to the waking state the dreams vanish.

Dreamless sleep

In the dreamless deep sleep state there is an absence of mental activity; there is no thinking, feeling, nor sensory perception. The individual is not conscious or aware of anything. But this is not negative, or a state of non-existence, for on waking we are happy and conscious of having slept a sound and restful sleep. We feel we existed even during sleep. In comparison to the waking and dreaming states of mental activity, whose characteristic is the presence of a knower and a known, or a thinker and a thought, in dreamless sleep the principle of consciousness remains and exits without its seeming to assume the duality of a conscious subject and object. Consciousness is continuous.

In deep dreamless sleep, the mental functions cease altogether, there is no thinker to think thoughts, there is no awareness of thoughts or 'I', there is no ego and no world. The Self recedes even from the mind. Both the five organs of perception, and the mind, remain hidden and latent, suspended in a state of ignorance (*ajñāna*), within the blissful sheath of the causal body.

During dreamless sleep the soul is united with consciousness, the nature of absolute bliss. But this is not the transcendental state or the fourth, known as *turīya*, in which the consciousness merges into the *ātmān* (Self). This union is only apparent, it is only a reflection; it is not the true union or superconsciousness that follows the knowledge and realisation of the Self. The sleeping individual returns to the consciousness of the waking state and returns to his conditioned personality, with the same habits, desires and attachments. The individual self remembers that it had a happy and sound sleep. This recollection results from experience therefore there must be experience in the deep dreamless sleep. The causal body, which is of the nature of ignorance (*avidyā*), veils the luminous self without affecting its innate blissfulness. Happiness becomes self-manifest being identical with consciousness that the Self is.

The difference between the dreamless sleep state and the transcendental state (*turīya*)

In both deep sleep and transcendental consciousness there is no consciousness of objects. But this objective consciousness is present in an unmanifested seed form in deep sleep while it is completely transcended in *turīya*. In *turīya*, the mind is not simply withdrawn from objects, but becomes one with *Brahman*.

The difference between sleep and death

In death there is a complete withdrawal of the organs into the heart-lotus or *Akasa* of the heart. But in the state of dream the organs are not absolutely withdrawn.

Sleep – a perfect model of death

At night, as we begin to fall asleep, we initially move into the hypnagogic state, where we start to relax and alpha waves become predominant. This is the state of quiet reverie, where many images and memories flash before the mind. As we continue to fall asleep we move into the deep sleep zone characterised by delta waves and further relaxation. In the next stage of sleep, the dream state, there is a deeper state of relaxation with rapid eye movement (REM), which is characterised by higher frequency alpha waves. The process of waking follows in the reverse order from REM sleep to deep sleep through the hypnagogic state to complete wakefulness.

Jagrat (waking state) – conscious mind – beta waves
Svapna (dream state) – subconscious mind – alpha and theta waves
Sushupti (deep sleep state) – unconscious mind – delta waves
Turīya (transcendental; superconsciousness) – unknown

In sleep or death we do not cease to exist, though all objective, individual experience has vanished. In sleep the mind and its thoughts and mental modifications assume a subtle state.

Dissolution of the body is no more than sleep. Just as a person sleeps and wakes up, so is death and birth. Death is like sleep. Birth is like waking up. The domain of sleep is partly the same domain as the transition into death. In both cases you enter the astral, but in death, it is generally done with more conscious awareness.

When a person goes to bed at night, he lies down and pulls the bed covers up to his neck to feel comfortable and cosy. Before he begins to fall asleep his mind is busy and restless with the worldly thoughts of the day – work, relationships, family, finances, etc. After some time his mind begins to settle down. Slowly his consciousness begins to withdraw. First it is only aware of the four walls of the bedroom. As he begins to feel sleepy, his consciousness begins to withdraw further so he is only aware of the bed and the covers. There is an involuntary relaxation of energy from the motor and sensory nerves, which causes the consciousness to further withdraw; the bed and covers are forgotten, he is mainly aware of his limbs, hands and feet. As the consciousness continues to recede, he is only aware of the centres of consciousness, from the navel to the brain. Gradually the senses withdraw from their respective objects. The sense organs cannot perceive their respective objects unless the mind joins with them. Truly speaking, it is the Self that perceives the objects through the mind and the sense organs. Then with his body lying still and relaxed he becomes only aware of the thoughts in the mind. After a while the conscious thoughts and activities of the mind settle down and completely withdraw, leaving the person fast asleep.

Sleep is a perfect model for explaining death for the process is very similar. We die every night in our sleep. It is almost like a preparation for death. In deep sleep the sense organs enter into the mind, and the soul withdraws into the subtle body. In death the soul abandons its physical sheath and is carried within the inner bodies – the subtle and causal bodies.

> *For me there is neither waking nor dream nor deep sleep, nor am I (the Self) conditioned by any of these three states; for these are all of the nature of nescience, but I am the fourth beyond these three. I am therefore the uncontradictable, attribute less Bliss.*
> Sri Sankaracharya

In sleep there is only sleep, not even 'I' who sleeps. You do not even know "I am asleep". That is, there is no experiencer independent of the experience. When there is no dream, no thought, nothing – no world – that is a complete deep sleep. The world disappears in relation to us and we are not conscious of any phenomena around us. All the persons and all our possessions, power and ego to which we are attached vanish and are forgotten in the state of deep sleep.

During the waking state a person's organs of perception, mind and the five *prāṇas*, though belonging to the subtle body, operate in the gross body. But in the dream state the organs of perception and the mind are withdrawn to the subtle body, and in dreamless sleep to the causal body. The five *prāṇas* continue to function in the gross body as in the waking state.

At death the organs, the mind, and the five *prāṇas* withdraw from the gross body and enter the subtle body, to which they belong. They all gather in the lotus-heart, where the subtle body in association with the Self is located.

In sleep, sleep alone exists, and therefore in sleep you are not aware that "I am" – otherwise you are awake! The sleeping person is not at all dissatisfied with this state of sleep, nor is there evidence that he is satisfied either. There is no dissatisfaction with that sleep, and no desire to wake up again.

The message of sleep is that it is possible for a person to remain totally absorbed, integrated with the state in which one is, without even an effort to get out of it, without a dissatisfaction arising from it, without a desire or craving for a state other than the one in which one is. When that is done there is no pain, there is no suffering. When one is in that integrated state where there is no conflict or division within oneself, then there is neither pain nor suffering.

The difference between personality and individuality

That which distinguishes a person from a thing or one person from another is personality. The term personality comes from the Latin word *persona*, 'the mask'. Personality is that particular consciousness which is ascribed to the physical body – descriptions that describe the physical status, name, character and emotional type, religion, profession – these labels are all attributed to the personality. They are the *persona*, 'the mask'.

Individuality is something that is beyond the gross body that is bound by time and space; it has no relation to the personality at all. Death destroys the personality but it cannot annihilate the individuality, the soul (Self). It is beyond the body and has a separate and distinct existence. The individuality is the sense of 'I' consciousness (the real Self) that has a continuous existence. It remains the same throughout childhood, youth and old age, and continues beyond.

The personality changes but the individuality, the sense of 'I' consciousness, never changes. It will continue to exist even after death. Even in the dream and dreamless states you have the sense of 'I' consciousness within. If you did not have the sense of 'I' in deep sleep you would not remember that you had a happy, sound sleep.

The individuality can only be lost when the individuality becomes one with the Supreme Self (*Para Brahman*) through deep meditation and the highest state of *samādhi* (superconsciousness), *Nirvikalpa Samādhi*, in which there is direct perception of the bliss of the soul or Self, and a total loss of any sense of duality. The soul is simultaneously conscious of Spirit within and of creation without. The soul wave (a reflection of Spirit) becomes the ocean of Spirit.

The reason why we find it so difficult to know the real Self is because we think in terms of describing it as an object, when we ourselves *are* it.

> *A man identifies himself about sixteen hours daily with his physical vehicle. Then he sleeps; if he dreams, he remains in his astral body, effortlessly creating any object even as do the astral beings. If man's sleep be deep and dreamless, for several hours he is able to transfer his consciousness, or sense of I-ness, to the causal body; such sleep is revivifying. A dreamer is contacting his astral and not his causal body; his sleep is not fully refreshing.*
> Swami Sri Yukteswar, from *Autobiography of a Yogi* by Paramhansa Yogananda

The essence of Consciousness – *Turīya* (the fourth)

Beyond the three states of consciousness – waking, dream, and dreamless sleep – is *Turīya*. This is the fourth state – Self-realisation. Truly speaking, *Turīya* is not a state at all, but the very nature and essence of our being, the Self. *Turīya* is present in all the states; it is Reality, pure consciousness in itself. The three states are subject to change, but the Self of an individual is distinct from all three states of existence, it is changeless. *Turīya*, the omnipresent

Consciousness, pervades all three states of existence; it is beyond time, space, and causation. The Self is the experiencer of the three states but remains unaffected by them. In the following verse from the *Māṇḍūkya Upaniṣad* (7), *turīya* is distinguished from the three states (waking, dream, dreamless sleep).

The Fourth (Turīya), the wise say, is not inwardly cognitive (as in the dream state), nor outwardly cognitive (as in the waking state); nor cognitive both ways (as in an intermediary state between waking and dreaming), neither is it an indefinite mass of cognition (as in dreamless sleep)*, nor collective cognition, nor unconsciousness. It is imperceivable, unrelated, inconceivable, uninferable, unimaginable, indescribable. It is the essence of the one self cognition common to all states of consciousness. All phenomena cease in it. It is peace, it is bliss, it is non-dual. That is the Self (ātmā), and That is to be realised.*

The States of Consciousness according to the *Māṇḍūkya Upaniṣad*

The entire range of human consciousness begins with the waking state and ends with the absolute state of superconsciousness, where all objective relations and perceptions of duality are completely negated. The spirit, both in its universal and individual aspects, becomes embodied and conditioned by *Prakṛiti* (eternal principle of matter) at three levels – causal, subtle, and gross. The spirit, covered by the three bodies (causal, subtle, and gross) is conditioned with three relative states of consciousness:

1. Gross or physical body – waking state (*jagrat*)
2. Subtle body – dream state (*svapna*)
3. Causal body – dreamless sleep (*sushupti*)

When the spirit is embodied in the universal aspect it is called macrocosm (universal consciousness). In the individual aspect it is called microcosm (individual consciousness).

The **Microcosmic** individual consciousness (*purusha* or *ātmān*) has four states of being:

Ātmān – the omniscient, eternal Self.

Prājñā – 'knower', undivided consciousness. Associated with *Īśvara* (God) – the source of all conscious souls.

Taijasa – 'luminous one'. The manifestation of the individual in the subtle body, that develops a false identification of the self with ego.

Viśva – the individual self, the experiencer of the waking state bound and conditioned by matter, and associated with the phenomenal world and the gross body.

The **Macrocosmic** universal consciousness (*Brahman*) also has four states:

Turīya or ***Avyakta*** – imperceptible and indescribable, absolute state beyond the three ordinary states of consciousness.

Īśvara – cosmic Lord or God, the omniscient source and cause of the universe. Associated with its own *maya* (illusory power) and the causal body.

Hiraṇyagarbha – cosmic Self. Also known as *Sutrātma* (thread-soul of the universe) because it binds all the constituents of the universe together.

Virāt – universal cosmic form. The fully manifested macrocosm encompassing all the aggregates of the perceptible and tangible phenomenal universe.

When *Turīya or Brahman* associates with its *maya* illusory power, it assumes the following three states – *jagrat* (waking), *svapna* (dream), *sushupti* (deep sleep):

Table 1: The States of Consciousness

State of Consciousness	**Microcosmic or individual**	**Macrocosmic**
Waking state (*Jagrat*)	*Viśva* Physical 'A' of AUM	*Virāt* (Cosmic manifestation)
Dream state (*Svapna*)	*Taijasa* Mental 'U' of AUM	*Hiraṇyagarbha* (Universal mind)
Sleep state (*Sushupti*)	*Prājñā* Intellectual 'M' of AUM	*Īśvara* (First cause or God)
Transcendental (*Turīya*)	Beyond the three states of ordinary awareness, yet pervading them all, is 'the fourth' (*turīya*), the *Brahman-ātmān*. *Turīya* is not a 'state' like the others, since it is present in all the states and is actually the whole reality, pure consciousness in itself.	

Part Three

The Self

What is Consciousness?

Divine Consciousness was described by Paramhansa Yogananda as, "centre everywhere, circumference nowhere." This, surely, is what Jesus meant also when he said, "Neither shall they say, Lo here! or, lo there! for, behold, the kingdom of God is within you."
Luke 17:21
Swami Kriyananda, *Revelations of Christ*, Crystal Clarity Publishers, Nevada City, CA, 2006

The mind is constantly fluctuating in thoughts, feelings, impressions, and states of waking, dreaming, and sleeping. Behind these mental fluctuations is a constant awareness, an unbroken sense of Self or being that continually observes and witnesses the mind's activities. When we are not caught up in our mental activity, but are attentively aware, our Self-awareness can perceive and observe the mind. You cannot be your thoughts, feelings, sensations, or anything else of an objective nature, because when they subside, you are present and aware of them. These thoughts, feelings, and sensations are transitory, they come and they go, but your real natural state or essential being – that single continuous consciousness in which the many and various aspects of objective experience come and go – is ever-present awareness that remains constant. It is all expansive without centre or periphery.

Consciousness-awareness is independent of the mind

Everyone knows that the drop is contained within the Ocean, but not everyone knows is that the Ocean is contained in the drop.
Kabir (1440–1518)

Waves appear on the sea, but they have no independent reality, they are just appearances of the underlying water; the wave has no independent existence as something apart from its source. Similarly, the body, mind and objects of the phenomenal world do not exist as independent realities; like the waves of the sea, they are manifestations or appearances of consciousness. Just as waves consist of water, all things objective consist of consciousness.

> *The Consciousness that is the Self is unchanging, but when it is reflected in the mind, the mind takes the form of that reflection and appears to be conscious.*
> Patañjali Yoga Sūtra 4:22

The principle of *awareness* is independent of the mind and its activities, just as water is independent of its fleeting manifestation of bubbles, ripples, and waves – these are nothing but water that rise and set. The water exists independently from the ripples and waves.

Without consciousness there is no world to witness or experience. Without the sense of 'I am', there can be no other experiences. That present awareness of 'I am' is your true nature. 'I' means consciousness. When you say, "I am", that 'am-ness' is the existence of that consciousness; it is the nature of oneself. *You are Consciousness. You are existence itself.* In any moment there is the ever-present opportunity or possibility for you to awaken to the truth of yourself as Consciousness by surrendering your mind to inner silence and stillness. The truth of who you are is *here* and *now*, the only thing that separates you from recognising the truth of who you are as the changeless, eternal Self is the belief in some thought that says you are not that. The obstacles to *realising* the truth are created in the activity of the mind – thoughts and feelings. It is the mind that causes you to feel separate. It is your past and future thoughts that have created the present thought of who you are, but the formless, changeless and limitless truth of your Reality is inseparable from any mental formulation of who you think you are.

To experience our thoughts and feelings requires the presence of *consciousness*. The phenomenal world, mind and body appear as objects within *consciousness*, within *awareness*. The fleeting objects of the world and the body and mind have no independent existence apart from being perceived in consciousness. Your body and mind are material objects that appear in consciousness; they do not exist as independent realities. The very nature of the mind is to express this awareness by means of name and form. You, the innermost Self, are the one to whom they appear. *Consciousness* is the eternal Reality alone that exists.

Consciousness is itself the proof of everything else

> *As light is the very nature of the Sun, coldness of water, heat of fire, so are being consciousness, bliss, eternity and absoluteness the very nature of the Self.*
> Sri Sankaracharya, *Select Works of Sri Sankaracharya*, translated by S. Venkataramanan, Pilgrims Publishing, Varanasi, India, 2005

In reality there is only non-dual Consciousness. Consciousness is a principle that does not have to be proved. It is itself the proof of everything else. Consciousness is self-existent. Those who experience consciousness in itself find that it is its own proof. Just as a light does not need the help of another light to show itself – its own light reveals it – so consciousness is its own proof. That Reality sees everything by its own light. It is Self-luminous.

The mind and consciousness are not in the brain

Essentially consciousness is not a mental state or mental process, but is *Awareness* itself: the Perceiver. If you were not aware you would not be able to take note of the mental and emotional states that you experience yourself in. So therefore, awareness cannot be a mental function; if it was it would disappear like all mental functions. Consciousness or awareness does not disappear, it is continuous and always present. The states you experience are *in* awareness.

Thinking and perceiving are functional consciousness which is discontinuous, but Pure Consciousness is the continuous Presence beyond time and space. You *are* that Pure Consciousness, it is your true nature and is always awake; it does not sleep. It is unconditional being and love.

Consciousness does not originate in the mind, nor the brain. The mind transmits the radiance of consciousness to the physical system. The brain being material is devoid of consciousness; it is only a medium or vehicle of consciousness, it is not its source. The mind is not in the brain. The brain is a physical organ, an instrument through which the mind works. This is why we say "my mind" – we view the mind as an instrument. The mind only appears to be conscious to us because the light of pure awareness or Pure Consciousness is reflected on to the mind. The mind itself has no awareness and is not self-luminous. All cognitions and feelings are expressions of inner Consciousness through different modes of the mind. Even our mental states are not conscious in themselves, but are illuminated by the light of the inner Consciousness, the luminous Self, just as coal becomes aglow when permeated by fire.

Being of the nature of consciousness, the Self is awareness itself. Consciousness is the being of the Self; it is the Knower, the eternal constant Witness which is permanent and unborn. It is the subject and never the object. It is Self-existent. We cannot deny it any more than we can deny ourselves, and deny existence.

Consciousness is ever present in us – in the waking, dream and sleep states. Waking consciousness and dream consciousness are but reflections of the light of the One Pure Consciousness in matter, in the form of the mind and the senses, in waking and dreaming.

Consciousness does not evolve but the mind does. The mind can evolve from being gross to subtle; it has the potential to become refined and cultured. It can also become pure and illumined (*sattvic*) by the spiritual disciplines and practices of Yoga and meditation, which help to remove the subconscious tendencies and impressions of the mind that keep us in ignorance of our true nature and identity.

Regaining your true blissful nature

To regain your true blissful nature, that divine and infinite Self, which is eternally yours, but is veiled by the three fundamental forces (the *guṇas* – *sattva*, *rajas*, and *tamas*), you have to reduce the *rajas-tamas* impurity, and increase the *sattvic* component of your nature. When Consciousness functions through a predominantly *sattvic* mind, It expresses Itself as the God-principle.

When your mind has learned *not* to dwell on matter or the objects of the senses, then your spiritual life has begun, not until then.

Unless your mind becomes fine and subtle, and *sattvic* (pure), you will not be able to detach from the endless desires and urges of the senses and their objects. You have to learn the art of quieting and stilling the mind, to go within, and feel and experience your own true essential nature as something different from the body, mind, and senses. When you are able to go into stillness, and your mind becomes calm, then you begin to experience Pure Consciousness (*Puruṣa*, the Self, *Ātmān*). When you discover your inner Consciousness then you will find spiritual Truth.

The Self and names and forms of objects

The great sage *Śankarācārya* (Sankaracharya), born in India around 820AD, tells us in his sacred scripture *Dṛg Dṛśya Viveka* that whatever exists is made up of five aspects.

> *Whatever exists has five aspects. Out of them, the first three – Existence, Knowledge and Bliss (Sat-Cit-Ānanda) – aspects point to Brahman as the unchanging One Reality. The other two: names and forms, point to the universe as multiplicity.*
> Dṛg Dṛśya Viveka, 20

These five aspects can be divided into two groups:

1. The eternal changeless *Brahman*, which is pure Being-Consciousness (*Sat-Cit-Ānanda*), the Ultimate Reality.
2. The universe of names and forms; the world of duality.

Names and forms of objects are only superimpositions on *Brahman*, the undifferentiated One Reality. Just as a pot is only a name of clay, a bracelet a name of gold, a cloth a name for threads, and sea and waves names for water.

One should discriminate between the One Reality (*Brahman*) and the superimposed names and forms of the world and universe. Then, having understood the real nature of the objects, the mind's attention can be withdrawn from the names and forms and absorbed in the One Reality, Pure Consciousness, the essence and source of all objects. When through *direct* experience you realise that other than Consciousness, there is no external world, then every experience in life can be used to return to the Source.

For an object to be seen there must be light (light of Consciousness), and the seeing is pointing to the Consciousness aspect of one's inner Self, just as the love that we feel for another person is the love inherent within us *as* our own Self.

Normally, when we look at an object we the mind instantly label and identify it with a name. When we see a tree, the mind says, "That is a pine tree," or "That is an oak tree." When we walk in a garden the mind is conditioned to label and identify every flower that it knows – "That is a yellow rose," "That is a pink carnation," and if we have studied flowers we may even go further and give its Latin name. The point is that by seeing in this way – by identifying and labelling everything we look at – we experience duality, we experience ourself as separate from the Totality.

The vast universe has projected outwards a multiplicity of infinite forms into our world. These forms are constantly changing; they have a beginning and an end. All forms and all perceptions arise in Consciousness, abide in Consciousness and merge in Consciousness. Therefore, Consciousness alone is real. Just as water is the background for seas, oceans and waves, so is Consciousness the background. Objects do not exist independently of thoughts. Without thought there is no object and thought itself is Consciousness. Beyond the mind, the objects become Consciousness itself. It is the mind that makes Consciousness appear as an object. Without labelling and identifying objective forms you come to realise that you are not your thoughts, but the *Knower* of your thoughts – the Seer, pure Consciousness – the screen on which all these thoughts are projected.

Seeing undivided Oneness

When looking at an object remove your seeing of the name and form, and be aware of its nameless nature, its reality as Consciousness. Seeing with awareness, effortlessly see the object with no intellectual thought of identifying it with a name or form. Make no judgement at all. Calmly look at the object for several minutes and experience the object as undivided Consciousness, as Oneness. Bring your attention back to its Source, so that the attention becomes present in both the object and the subject. The Seer merges into seeing and seeing merges into the seen as One. Only Awareness (the Self, pure Consciousness) remains as the Seer, the seen, and the seeing.

The real nature of who I am

> *That which is denoted by the word "I" forever remains sole and transcendental. That which is gross, undergoes multiplicity. How then can the body be the Self?*
> Sri Sankaracharya

Am I the body?

The body is objective, it is known to you – you see it, feel it and sense it, therefore it cannot be the subject 'I', 'you' the individual.

If you say, "I am the body," you will also identify with other characteristics of the body, such as "I am young," "I am strong," "I am British," "I am an artist." But what is the body? The body is material, subject to change and impermanence. The cells of the body are constantly undergoing change. Ninety-nine per cent of your body is composed of the elements of oxygen, carbon, hydrogen, nitrogen, calcium and phosphorus, and about 0.85% is composed of potassium, sulphur, sodium, chlorine and magnesium. The elements, body cells and all matter on the Earth is made of atoms, which are made up of smaller particles of electrons, protons and neutrons. These are made up of even smaller particles called quarks and leptons (the building blocks of atoms, protons and neutrons). You have billions of billions of atoms in your body, but the atoms your body is made of now are not the same atoms that you were made of 10 or 20 years ago. The atoms that make up your body now will not care when they are no longer part of you. So if your body no longer contains even a single atom that made you when you were a child, are you the same person? Was that you, back then, or is this you now?

Look at a family photograph album of yourself or family relation. See how the body has changed from being a baby, a child, a youth, to middle age and old age.

In your deep dreamless sleep you were not aware of your body, and there was no sense of 'I', the ego-self.

As a body you are in space, as mind you are in time. Both the body and mind are entirely dependent on Consciousness. The body and mind are constantly changing and they come into existence only when you think of them.

Am I the physiological functions of the body?

Every day we attribute the 'I' to various conditions when we say, "I am thirsty," "I am hungry," "I am ill," or "I am healthy." All these conditions are known to you, and they are not permanent. You know when you are hungry and when you are not hungry, so since you know both these conditions, you are neither of them.

Am I the senses?

"I see," "I hear," "I taste," "I smell." You experience the world of many and varied objects through your senses, which objectifies them.

When I see, I am the seer; when I hear, I am the hearer; when I taste, I am the taster; and when I smell, I am the smeller. It seems as though the 'I' is placed in the eyes, ears, tongue and nose, because consciousness seems to be present in the eyes, ears, tongue and nose.

But even if any of the senses are not functioning, you are still aware of them functioning or not functioning. So you cannot be the senses.

Behind the senses is the mind, which has the power to transmit consciousness, the 'I' (the Self or *Ātmān*), the knower, that gives light to the mind. The senses cannot perform their cognitive tasks without the presence of consciousness in all of them. Objects depend upon consciousness but consciousness – the *Knower* behind all perception – does *not* depend upon objects. Objects are never separated from their respective sense organ, even in thought. What we perceive is the superimposition of the senses and mind upon their separate objects. It is only the witnessing Consciousness, the 'I'-principle that *knows.*

Am I the mind?

The mind is always objectifying. It is an instrument of knowing; without the mind the eyes cannot see, the ears cannot hear, the tongue cannot taste, and the nose cannot smell. The mind is present in the perceptions of seeing, hearing, tasting, smelling and touching.

The mind is present in the waking and dream states but not in the deep dreamless state. The mind is comprised of thoughts and feelings; without them it has no real existence, it is impermanent and transitory. Beyond the mind, there is only Consciousness (Self, the 'I'-principle). The mind disappears with the cessation of thoughts, while the changeless infinite Self remains as the Witness-Awareness. *You*, the Self are eternal.

Emotions/feelings

The mind has the functions of thinking and feeling. The mind is either thought itself or feeling itself, but when they are not present there is no mind, it does not exist.

The mind not only objectifies the various objects, but also desires them. You cannot feel or will without cognition. The mind responds to the objects and situations emotionally – "I am happy," "I am sad," "I am angry," "I am frightened," "I am restless" are all emotions or feelings that frequently change. They are not my true nature because I am the one who observes the momentary changes of emotions. I am aware that sometimes I am sad and sometimes happy. So I cannot be the emotions.

View your emotions/feelings as the witnessed. You are the disinterested silent witness. You can also observe the emotion/feeling rising in you, abiding in you and disappearing into you, knowing that is made of your real nature (Consciousness) itself.

Intellect

The intellect is the thinking or discriminating faculty; it is the capacity of the mind to know objects and concepts. The knowledge of a tree is known by you through a thought of the object 'tree' occurring in your mind. All knowledge of tangible objects, ideas or concepts occurs in the mind, but this cognition comes and goes, so I cannot be the very thought which leads to a discovery of something, because even without this thought of discovery leading to the knowledge of an object, idea or concept, 'I', the knower or consciousness, was aware of it.

Memory

Memory – a function of the mind – functions by remembering and recalling past thoughts, activities and events; it merges the past into the present. I gather and recollect memories of my childhood and I remember what I did yesterday; I can recollect the experiences of where I travelled and what I did, and the emotions and feelings I felt. Over time memories fade, disappear or become distorted; it is impossible to remember everything accurately. I cannot be my memories, since I am aware of all thoughts related to my past. The perceived cannot be the perceiver; whatever you see, hear, think, or remember, you are not that. A thought is recalled by that principle which perceived it at the time of its occurrence. Therefore, it is the 'I'-principle, the changeless witness, that always knows the mental activities, and recalls a thought at any point in time. The ego remembers the past thought while the real 'I'-principle witnesses it all.

Thoughts

The variable thoughts (uncertainties, doubts, fears, etc) rise in the mind because there is a thinker – the I-thought or ego, which is the mind. As a thought rises in the mind, it exists momentarily and gives way to a new thought. One thought is replaced by another thought, but the content of both thoughts is invariable. Every thought that comprises of emotions, intellect, ego and memories depends upon Consciousness, the 'I'-principle beyond time, for its existence.

Thoughts rise, exist and disappear into Consciousness, just as waves rise, exist and disappear in the sea. And just as waves are made of water, the content of thoughts is Consciousness.

If a thought arises, to whom does it occur? It is not the body, because it is inert matter, and it is not the mind because the mind itself is a thought, and one thought cannot occur to another thought.

Objects do not exist independently of thoughts. Without thought there can be no object, and thought is itself Consciousness. The 'I'-Consciousness alone *knows* thoughts, but does not express itself. To correlate two thoughts the mind is utilised. The mind identifies itself with the 'I', working in the name of 'memory'.

All thoughts arise from the ego. The ego-self is transitory, whereas the real Self (Consciousness) is eternal, changeless and permanent. So 'I' who am beyond the mind as Consciousness, that thoughts occur, cannot be the thoughts.

Thought has no intelligence of its own. Its movement is limited by its identity and its own programming. It is conditioned by the past. Thought is dualistic; it separates, divides, and fragments the Oneness of Life into 'things'. All words are based on concepts and ideas. Thought expresses itself through concepts, images, symbols, opinions, beliefs, memories and ideas. Thought is always a movement away from the truth of what *is*; from *awareness*. As a movement in the mind, thinking distorts the capacity to perceive clearly, for when everything is in harmony thought ceases, therefore the occurrence of thinking indicates some aspect must be attended to. In order for a thought to be perpetuated, it needs to be thought about – a thought forms a relationship with an existing thought to perpetuate itself.

The tendency of the mind is to be captivated and entertained by the expressions of thought by thinking. When thinking occurs recognise the fact of thinking without becoming involved in the content of the thinking. View your thoughts as the *witnessed*. You are the disinterested silent *Witness*. This quality of disinterest allows you to perceive the movement implicit in the expression.

Ego

The ego is thc I-thought; the true or real 'I' is the changeless Self (Consciousness). Egoism is misidentification of one's self with the body, senses and mind. In deep dreamless sleep the I-thought or ego does not exist. All struggle comes from the ego's determination to sustain its separate identity. The ego clings on to its accumulated memories, or projects desires into the future.

In any activity there seems to be two 'I's functioning at the same time: the ever-changing ego or false 'I' as the doer; and the real 'I'-Consciousness, the changeless Self as the *Knower*. The real 'I' or changeless Self is present in all actions and states, even in deep sleep.

Therefore your real subjective nature of *Being* is always the *Knower Consciousness* and never the objective doer/enjoyer.

'I'-consciousness – I am, I exist

I am not the body and its functions, I am not the senses, I am not the mind and its functions – thoughts, emotions, feelings, intellect, and memories. After discarding all that is not-self (body, mind and senses) is the permanent, changeless principle – the infinite Self, *Sat-Cit-Ānanda* (Ever-existent, Ever-conscious, Ever-new Bliss). I am the subject, the individual conscious Being-Awareness who is aware of the body, senses and mental activities. This Being-Awareness, the 'I'-consciousness, has the ability to know the internal activities of the body, mind and senses, and the capacity to know external things. This changeless subjective principle 'I'-consciousness is present throughout all the three states: waking, sleep and dream. It is this 'I', the changeless reality, that witnesses and experiences the waking (*jagrat*), dream (*svapna*) and sleep (*sushupti*) states. It is only in the conscious wakeful state that you are aware of the world and its sufferings; in the deep dreamless sleep you are not aware.

My Kriya Yoga teacher, Swami Kriyananda (1926–2013), pointed out to me that the French philosopher René Descartes was mistaken in his famous declaration, "I think; therefore I am." His error lay in the fact that consciousness *precedes* thought: it is not a *product* of mentation. Deep awareness demands a suspension of the thinking process. It would be truer to restate Descartes thus, "I am (aware of being), therefore I think."

You may have doubts about many things, but at any moment in time you cannot deny that you exist – *"I am," "I exist"* – because *you* the experiencer must be present in order to deny it. No one would deny their own existence. Would you look in a mirror to know that you exist? You know that you exist and always know that *"I am."* Existence is knowledge and awareness – *"I am the Knower, I know my actions, perceptions, thoughts and feelings and I know myself."*

You exist, always changeless, whether perceptions occur or not. The body, senses and mind are your objects. You the 'I'-principle are the conscious-aware subject; the ultimate Witness (silent awareness) to all your activities. All objects, thoughts and feelings are known through the senses or the mind, but *you* the Witness, the Consciousness in all activities, always know through *direct knowledge* that *"I am." "I am the Knower"* of the body, senses and mind. Therefore, because the 'I'-principle (the witnessing Consciousness; the Self) is present in all these activities, you are evidently distinct and separate from them all. Consciousness is always your centre in all activities; it cannot be otherwise. In every activity on the plane of the mind-body experience, the 'I'-principle, Consciousness, is the *Witness* that perceives the mind.

The Self that I am cannot be thought of because *I am* the Self, that is my real nature. Consciousness is perceiving. I cannot perceive the perceiving because I am *it.* Things depend upon varying proofs to establish their existence, but the 'I' (Consciousness) is self-evident, it is self-luminous (*svayam-prakāsha*), it is the light of lights, it does not require any other light for its manifestation.

What am I? I can perceive and know my body, sense organs, and mind, and my actions, perceptions, thoughts and feelings are known to me. Therefore, I am evidently the subject, distinct and separate from all of them.

Knowingly or unknowingly, it is the Reality of one's own real nature (*svarūpa*) – Existence, Consciousness and Bliss – that we are all seeking. When this is limited by the mind it becomes life, thought and feeling. *Knowingness* is your real nature, it is never separated from you – just as 'radiating light' of the sun is its real nature, it ceaselessly shines.

All effort, including Yoga techniques and meditation, is only to remove the physical and psychological obstacles that stop you from establishing yourself in the Truth.

The truth of the Self is not something you have to acquire, or to go in search of – it already *is*. The Self or Consciousness is the very core of your *being*. It does not require any other light, because it is self-luminous. Recognise and accept it and become established in it, so it becomes your natural state. Be centred in Consciousness. Nothing can limit Consciousness; you are unlimited.

Awareness

> *Everything in existence, including (as a logical necessity) every creature and every ego-motivated human being, has its reality only as a manifestation of Infinite, Self-Aware Bliss. The goal of all striving cannot be anything but reabsorption into the Infinite Self.*
>
> Swami Kriyananda, *Revelations of Christ*, Crystal Clarity Publishers, Nevada City, CA, 2006

There is something which is *aware* in this present moment. It is prior to all thoughts, feelings and sensations of the body. What is it? What is that awareness which is aware now?

When you can quieten your mind, so that all thoughts cease from arising and you still remain conscious and alert, then you can recognise that without thoughts you are still *present here* and *now*. You recognise the ever-present awareness *you* are. You are obviously not your thoughts – you must be the *awareness itself*. That awareness is Consciousness itself – that awareness, that *Consciousness*, is your essential nature that is ever-present and continuous in all three states (waking, dream, sleep). Awareness always *is*. It is also the witness of all your activities, or inactivities, in each state. All states that you experience move in and out of awareness, but awareness remains unchanged by any state that appears in awareness. The truth of who you really are does not come and go. It is continuous, present before birth, throughout your life, and after death. Consciousness always is; it does not come into existence in time.

Being present means to be totally and unconditionally *aware* of your aliveness in the present moment. Consciousness asserts and proves that you are not the doer or enjoyer, but that you are always the witnessing *awareness*, the *knower*.

Remember, know and realise your real nature now

You need to constantly remind yourself that you are not the body, senses, mind, thoughts and feelings, and personality. You are not the 'I'-thought, it is not the real 'I'. Remember, know and realise that 'I' is Consciousness itself. Pure Consciousness, deep peace, happiness and bliss are your *real* nature – your innermost Self, which is existing eternally here and now, beyond all states. Transcending the body, senses and mind, *"I know I am."*

To experience your real nature of *Sat-Cit-Ānanda* (ever-existent, ever-conscious, ever-new Bliss), the real changeless 'I'-principle, you must transcend the body, senses and mind and the objective world. Remove the thought aspect from the 'I'-thought, and what remains is the permanent background to all thoughts – the real '*I*', or '*I am*' – your innermost Self. The thoughts and the world can only shine by your light. The changeless 'I' is the self-luminous principle. During your daily activities try to remain Self-aware of that changeless 'I'-principle, while knowing that the activities – action, perception, thought and feeling – themselves are changing every moment, and are not part of your real nature.

By affirming *"I am Pure Consciousness"* the 'I' and 'Consciousness' cannot be objectified, therefore this affirming thought or contemplation can never draw you outward away from your centre; it drives away all intruding thoughts and can only take you inward, ultimately merging in the Consciousness (the Self).

Affirm your real nature: *"Śivōham, Ānandōham"* – *"I am Pure Consciousness, I am Bliss."*

"I am Sat-Cit-Ānanda" (ever-Existent, ever-Conscious, ever-new Bliss).

Time and Space

To understand time and space we need to understand what is Consciousness, for we live, move and have our being in Consciousness. Consciousness is the essence – a living principle in which the entire cosmos is the projection and play of the all-pervading Consciousness that is vibrating with timeless Cosmic Energy. Consciousness manifests itself in every form – gross and subtle. Consciousness is the Ocean in which all waves rise, exist and dissolve.

The concept of time can be either objective or subjective. Anything you objectify is evident to you including time and space, either by direct perception or inference. Consciousness is always present in the object and the subject – they are sustained by Consciousness. *'I am'*, 'I'-Consciousness *is*, and everything else is an object of Consciousness. *You* the 'I'-consciousness are not subject to time or limited to space. Your real nature is *Sat-Cit-Ānanda*, which means you are not limited by time, you are ever-Existent (*Sat*), you are ever-Conscious (*Cit*), and you are that expansive ever-new Joy or Bliss (*Ānanda*). That is your real essential nature.

Space and Time are Consciousness

Both space and time are Consciousness, but Consciousness is not time and space, it is not located in a place. It cannot be measured, or limited in any way. Consciousness is spatially limitless and timeless.

We suffer not only through identification with our body, senses and mind, but also through living in time. Identifying with time brings with it – change, anxiety, hope and fear. Past is memory and the future is imagination mixed with promise, doubt, hope and fear.

The present has no time; it is *here* and *now*. The present has no movement; it is only your mind that is in movement. When your mind is still – uncluttered by thoughts about *me*, what *I* believe, *my* past and future, *my* likes and dislikes and what *I* want – time ceases, past and present merge into the eternal now. Just as every wave subsides into the ocean, so does every moment return to its source. Discovering the Source and abiding there is Self-realisation. Who you really are can only be experienced in this present moment. The true happiness, peace, love, joy and contentment you are searching for is not in time, but is *now* in the present moment. Happiness, peace, love, joy and contentment are not something to be achieved for they are your very nature, your very *Being*. It is yours already. Wanting happiness, peace, love and contentment implies that you do not already have them and so you feel limited in time. You live in hope that the future will bring you happiness, peace, love and contentment, and you continue to experience struggle, conflict, effort, restlessness and dissatisfaction. But your essential nature – the indwelling changeless Self, the 'I'-Consciousness – *is* the experience of freedom, happiness, peace, contentment and joy. It all depends on whether you are identified with the limitations of the ego-mind or with the changeless Self that is *Sat-Cit-Ānanda*. Are you aware of and attentive to the *present* moment, abiding in the reality of the inner Self? Or are you caught in time (*past* and *future*), in the habitual patterns of thinking, feeling and memories that become your ego-personality?

Thought in space and time

Thought is not limited by space but it is limited by time. Thought arises from memory (a record of whatever is happening) and memory is always related to time. Thought is never new. In its development thought gives rise to the thinker.

Time is the illusion of duration created by the parallel movement of the thinker/thought and an outer thought/form (an object or image). By duplicating within itself the movement of an outer occurrence the mind creates the feeling of duration. There is no time or space outside identification or relationship.

Time and space do not exist in deep sleep

In deep sleep there is no conception of time. You do not know where you are or what the time is. Where there is no conception of time, causality and ignorance cannot exist, for in deep sleep there is only peace, undisturbed by any other experience.

After waking from deep sleep we assert: "I slept peacefully, I do not know anything." In the deep sleep experience time, space and your individuality disappears, but you the 'I'-principle (Consciousness) was there to witness it. That is why, when you wake up from a good night of sleep, you say, "I slept peacefully." There was no awareness of time or space. In deep sleep the real 'I' exists all alone, without any other object. Your true changeless Self, the limitless Consciousness, the ever-present *Witness* is present in deep sleep, and in the dream and wakeful states. But in deep sleep there is no awareness of time and space, and in dream you create an illusion of time, which disappears as soon as you wake from dream sleep. Then, *You* the Conscious Awareness become aware of the disappearance of time. The presence of Consciousness is the timeless *'now'*, the present moment.

The dream world in which you are only half-awake rises from your knowledge, but in a dream you cannot create an object that you have never seen before; you cannot think of what you do not know.

Unlimited by Time and Space

When you identify yourself with only the mind-body, you become bound and limited by time and space. Your essential nature – the ever-present changeless Self – is *free* – you are not subject to time and not subject to any spatial limitation – but your present awareness of that freedom remains restricted by the belief that you are absolutely separate. The truth and eternal reality is that you cannot ever be separate from that *pure changeless ever-present awareness* that you are. The unreal comes and goes in time and space, but you, the 'I'-Consciousness, the Reality that is expressing life through the mind-body, is ever-existent, ever-conscious and not limited by time or space at all. The Self, pure Consciousness or Truth, is timeless and limitless, beyond the conceptual boundaries and limits created by the mind.

God, Time and Space

All theistic religions maintain that God or Spirit is present everywhere at the same time – God is omnipresent. The word 'everywhere' implies space. God is inherent in this space that is everywhere. Wherever there is space God is there – within us and outside of us. All that we perceive is that Divine Consciousness (God). Space is not different from or separate from God. Space and time are part of creation and the Creator, who is all intelligence, all knowledge and all power and is not separate from creation. For instance, your house is outside and you are inside, but both the house and you are within space.

The only obstacle to not perceiving the presence of God or our true divine nature is our restless, scattered and changing mind that through wrong identification with the body, senses and mind makes us feel separate and finite. Such a scattered and objective mind cannot give you the truth; you forget your own real nature (ultimate Reality). Your personality is always changing but your real individuality is changeless.

That Divine Consciousness that we call God permeates everything that exists. God is in space but is *not* space, and God being the 'Eternal One' is beyond time, for eternity is beyond time.

God is Self-conscious, All-conscious *Being*; there is absolutely no limitation. God is infinite, eternal Being, which exists independent of all changes that occur in time and space. There is no duality in God.

Space is not different from or separate from God. Both space and time are a part of creation.

Eternity is not within time

The concept and ultimate goal of most religions of going to heaven – a location, an outer paradise, that you go to for your merits, as a result of your *karma* – cannot be an eternal heaven, because eternity is not within time. Jesus Christ taught that the kingdom of heaven is within us. The Self is the kingdom of heaven or God because the Self is all there is; there can be no within or without because there is nothing outside the Self. To realise the kingdom of God all that is required is to be still and present in the moment, and know your divine changeless Self. The divine Self, *'I am'*, which is your Divinity, is not something which is attained in the future, for it is ever-present. The moment you know this Truth, that you are what you are searching for, you will remain still.

Time is the object of Consciousness, which is ever-present as the Self. Time is based on the ideas of past, present and future, and therefore it has no existence without the mind thinking of it. Thought depends upon time for its existence, and time depends upon thought. Thought tries to connect the past and the present. The past and the future both depend upon the present for their existence, but neither the past nor the present can be brought to the present, therefore time is non-existent. When you arrest the flow of thoughts, you will realise the non-existence of time and space – *"Be still and know that I am God"* – once you become aware of the Self, you will realise the consciousness and presence of God in everything.

'Now' – the present moment

Timelessness is always in the 'now' present moment. Consciousness (the Self, the 'I'-principle, the *ātmān*) which is limitless is *not* limited or bound by space or time.

The past was always present. The energies which formed a past moment have reformed to create the present. There is no past, only memories. These memories merely reflect that aspect of a past moment to which you were inattentive, that aspect which was not fully absorbed.

Thought depends upon time for its existence. Thought is always a movement to the past or the future; it is never in the present of what *is*. It is only in the aware and attentive mind that thought does not arise in the present. Thoughts are invariably about unresolved past situations, or the perpetuation of past momentum into the future.

Being *present* is one of the secrets to happiness. Your attentive *awareness* determines your experience of reality. Being *present* to what you are doing in every moment quietens the mind of its incessant thinking by allowing you to experience life as it is unfolding. You are not your thoughts, feelings, memories, opinions, beliefs and desires – they are part of the conditioned ego mind. You are the *Consciousness* which is *aware* of the thoughts not the thinker who is thinking them.

The hindrances to realising the Self

The hindrances to realising the Self, your real nature, are past memories, desires, accumulated tendencies (*vāsanās* and *saṁskāras*), habits of thoughts, and wrong identification of the Self with the non-self. It is because you identify your Self with the names, forms, and activities of the mind and body, that you remain unaware of your true nature.

In the Bible (Psalms 46:10), it says: *"Be still and know that I **am** God."* To be still is to have a quiet mind free from thought. To know that "I am" is the Reality, the Truth. That Reality is always present *here* and *now* as the conscious Self within you. The seat of realisation is *within* you as the Self; it is not an object that can be found outside of you. Your *awareness* is proof that you exist but you confuse it with the fluctuating mind with its myriad of thoughts, impressions and images, and with the body, the receptor of sensory experience. Even during sleep you still exist – just as the sun is always present and shining even when obscured by dark clouds in the day or by the darkness of night – the 'I'-principle is always self-evident, present as Consciousness, as the transcendent indivisible

One Witness. Unlike the mind, the Self never undergoes modifications. Duality is only in manifestation as the body, senses and mind. It is the Self alone that illumines the mind, intellect and sense organs. You see the mind's activity by the light of the Self; it is a mistake to think that the Self can be known by the mind or intellect, for the Self alone has the power to perceive the Self – its nature is *Knowledge* itself.

Ignorance (*avidyā*) is the obscuring dark cloud which conceals and prevents the true light of the Self (*Ātmān*) from shining through. When the infinite Self, your permanent reality, is revealed, ignorance vanishes, just as a cloud is dispelled by the light of the sun.

Part Four

Meditation, the Path to Inner Peace and Bliss

While others waste their time, meditate,
and you will see in meditation
that Silence will speak to you.
Paramhansa Yogananda

Know your true purpose in life

In this technological/digital age our culture is orientated toward action: an outward seeking, enjoying sense fulfilment, that continually keeps us distracted and preoccupied. No time is made for inner reflection and meditation. We have become so separated from our own real nature that we do not believe there can be anything particularly interesting or valuable within us. So, instead of meditating most people fill their free time with watching television or videos, or playing and socialising using their latest digital gadgets – iPad, laptop, or mobile phone – keeping them in a constant state of restlessness, disturbing their inner balance, and keeping them in forgetfulness of their own true nature, the forgetting of the infinite, transcendental quality of Reality. The identification of oneself with that state of forgetfulness produces a sense of separateness and otherness or non-Self. The mind identified with the sense of otherness becomes busy trying to repossess this 'other' through worldly sense experiences. This creates a self-division in your Being, and because you believe that you are not complete in yourself and that there is something else to attain, you continually chase after that 'other', trying to possess it to gain satisfaction and fulfilment.

The sense of fulfilment, completeness, balance, and happiness that we are all seeking is experienced when we set aside the daily demands and distractions of the world that claim our attention, and go within in the stillness of deep meditation.

The three main purposes toward finding true inner and outer fulfilment in life

1. To seek and find true lasting happiness
2. To realise your full human potential
3. To balance the material and spiritual aspects of your life

When you have the right understanding that the purposes of all experiences are to stimulate and encourage your spiritual development, then you have the right attitude to life and to meditation.

If you do not know your higher purpose in life, meditation and inner reflection will help to reveal it. Then you will be able to unfold your innate qualities, and awaken your inner potential. Paramhansa Yogananda said: *"Focus your attention within. You will experience new power, new strength, and peace in body, mind, and spirit. All limitations will be vanquished."*

Beginning to meditate

Beginning to meditate can be likened to starting a long journey, a pilgrimage into the mind itself. It is a spiritual journey to the source of your Being. This journey begins when you start to become aware that there must be a higher Consciousness, a Truth to be realised, an inner spiritual goal as opposed to an outer material goal. The journey begins when the material world starts to lose its attraction for you. It is then that you start seeking through philosophy, religion, or spirituality answers for the questions: "Who am I?" "What is the purpose of my life?" "How can I be free of suffering?" "Who or What is God?" "What happens to me after death?" We read books, and ponder on these philosophical questions. We seek out wise teachers or gurus who perhaps may be able to answer these profound questions. We may pray for the answers, or we may even doubt for a while that there is a Truth or God to be realised. But this is the beginning, generally, where most of us start our spiritual journey of meditation. It is a process of emptying the mind of all that is of the non-Self, all the conditioning, ideas, and wrong thinking, that is not our true divine nature. You have to empty yourself fully before the pure superconscious energies can freely flow through you. Having reached this state of emptiness and sincere searching, you soon start to realise the futile attempt to find Truth and happiness on the outside. Then you will begin to know that Reality, or the Self God, resides within you, and you must go within yourself to realise it.

Our spiritual journey is not always an easy one. Just by choosing to lead a spiritual life, we are swimming against the current. The world around us is flowing in one direction but we have decided to go in another. Most people in the world are identified with their body, mind and personality characteristics, resulting in a false sense of separation from their true divine nature. By entering the spiritual path of meditation we have decided to remove this delusive error of perception by having direct knowledge of the Truth, Reality, or Self-God, to experience directly in meditation what we are as pure existence-being. When you accept this fundamental position that your present state is a state of ignorance (*avidyā*), then it is clear that your true purpose and effort should be given to spiritual life, because spiritual life is the life that is dedicated to the finding of eternal Truth, the ultimate Reality, in which we find ultimate fulfilment.

The moment you find that there is something 'missing' from your life and that there must be something higher and superior to your present existence, then you begin to question your present way of living and your own existence, and you try to rise up to it. But of course you cannot immediately rise to higher consciousness, because you are deeply conditioned by past habits; and without earnestness and sincerity to know the ultimate Truth and a strong persistent effort to extricate yourself from conditioned thought and habit you will not succeed easily.

In the early stages of your spiritual life it is quite likely that you will be faced with situations that show you what you need to work on – attachments you feel to desires of the world, strong inclinations of the ego, and dislikes toward certain things and certain people – that will test your ability to maintain right attitude. Your habits will probably be undisciplined and willpower ineffective. Old patterns of thoughts and emotions will surface which you will need to transform. You will have to mould the areas that are different into a new lifestyle so that there will be nothing in your subconscious mind that opposes what is in the conscious or superconscious mind. It is only when all three of these areas of consciousness act in harmony that meditation can be truly attained and sustained. In other words, you will have to reprogramme your subconscious mind to change it through positive thinking, positive affirmations and setting positive spiritual goals that will strengthen your will. As soon as strong initiative is taken to refine your personality, a new inner process will begin to take place within you.

The Power of Affirmation: A powerful tool for inner and outer transformation

The first step toward Self-realisation is bringing your mind into balance and harmony with your true inner Self, and re-establishing your wholeness with life. This requires a self-education on your part: a self-awareness, an attentiveness to life from moment to moment.

The truth and reality remain hidden from us because for too long we have identified our Self with the mind and ego-personality, which have a limited vision of reality. It is only through false identification of the Self with the ego-mind-personality that ignorance exists – "I am this body," "I am this personality," "This is mine." As soon as you drop this false idea and regain your true identity as pure consciousness, the eternal, blissful Self, then ignorance and the ego of separateness disappear.

Your everyday thoughts, words and actions create your habits, desires, behaviours, emotions, feelings, attitudes and sense-urges. These in turn shape and mould your life into the personality and character that you have made for yourself. Your thoughts shape your destiny. You are what you think, not only consciously but also subconsciously. For years you have repeated words and statements, and attached meaning to them with your thoughts and feelings, which have created latent seed impressions (*saṁskāras*) in the soil of your subconscious mind. These impressions sink into the subconscious mind from the conscious mind and remain there, holding you in your conflicting patterns of feeling, habit and reaction.

The subconscious records all of what you think and believe, whether you want it or not. You give out the orders and the subconscious carries them out. Every act and every condition has its origin in the mind. Thoughts, whether positive or negative, are seeds that, when dropped or planted in the subconscious mind, germinate, grow and produce their fruit in due season.

Your thoughts can change your life

To change the conflicting subconscious patterns of thoughts and feelings of fear, worry and sorrow, and negative attitudes and habits, you can use the power of positive affirmation. An affirmation is a powerful tool that you can utilise to transform and change the course of your life. Affirmations are statements of truth-positive words, that are regularly repeated verbally and mentally for the purpose of confirming what is true, or of what you want to be true; or awakening to what is desirable. They help to positively change and update your belief systems. Each affirmation of spiritual truth connects you more completely with the power of God within you, allowing you to perform your creative role more effectively.

By thinking positively you will gain self-confidence and will have the power to be more effective when dealing with challenges and problems as they arise in your life. Positive thinking, willingness to see things in a new way, and using positive affirmations will help you to conquer whatever negative and stressful thoughts are keeping you feeling defeated, worried, fearful and unhappy. Positive affirmation gives you empowerment, and with this inner affirmative power and awareness no external condition or circumstance can hold you in bondage.

Affirmations are always worded to describe ideal circumstances as existing in the present. You affirm what *is*, not what you hope for.

Using the words 'I am' with clarity and purpose

When you begin a sentence with "I am" it gives power to your statement. The statement can be negative "I am unhappy" or positive "I am happy." When saying "I am" you need to be careful to follow it with only the positive thoughts, feelings, characteristics and conditions with which you want to be identified.

Most of us give hardly any thought to *who* the "I" actually refers to, and by declaring such statements – "I am unable," "I am poor," "I am incapable" – with such limited focus we block and limit ourselves.

Now rephrase those three statements into positive thoughts and see how they empower you – "*I am able* to accomplish my highest aim and purpose in life," "*I am* open to God's creative flow of abundance," "*I am* capable of overcoming life challenging situations, inner wisdom reveals divine solutions." In rephrasing the negative to positive statements you affirm your *confidence* and assert your *willingness* by connecting to the Truth within you.

I AM That I AM

The Truth of who you are – I AM – the Consciousness, Spirit, Christ, God-Self. The I AM is beyond all names and forms. It is the presence and power that links us to God. It gives life to and expression through the body, but it transcends the body. It is not your true identity.

Throughout the Bible there are various references to the I AM principle which designates the individualised Presence, the divine Self within each of us:

Be still and know that I AM.
Psalm 46:10

On that day my people shall know my name;
that I AM is the one who speaks.
Isaiah 52:6

I tell you the truth, before Abraham was born, I AM.
The words of Jesus in John 8:57

I AM the bread of life. Anyone who eats this bread
will live forever. And the bread that I shall give
is my flesh, for the life of the world.
John 6:51

I AM the good shepherd.
John 10:11

And God said to Moses: "I AM that I AM."
Exodus 3:14

In the Bible Gospels Jesus Christ perfectly expressed the I AM presence of God within him. Jesus uses I AM numerous times to indicate his identity with God (the Father), not as an ego-identification of his own specialness, but in expressing God's Power working through him, by uniting his individual will with God's supreme Will, for without God's Power he can do nothing.

The ego says "I am this or "I am that," but the spiritually awakened who have transcended the limited and vain ego affirm as Jesus did, when he fully expressed the Christ Presence within him and said:

The words that I speak to you are not just my own.
Rather, it is the Father, who dwells in me doing His work.
John 14:10

I AM in my Father, and you in me, and I in you.
John 14:20

The Father is greater than I.
John 14:28

The Father and I are One.
John 10:30

In another verse in John 7:33, Christ says to the Jewish Pharisees and the guards that came to arrest him: *"Where I AM you cannot come."* The Jews could not understand the meaning in his words, for they were limited by their own ego-consciousness. Interpreted in another way, Christ is saying that in that Presence where I AM, the Source of Divine Being and Truth, no one who is separate from that Source can come. Only those who are living in the divine consciousness of the I AM, the eternal Presence, the Source of Life know and understand the meaning of these words.

Jesus said to him: "I Am the way and the Truth and the Life.
No one comes to the Father except through me."
John 14:6

Identification of the Self (I AM) with personality and its projections is the root cause of all suffering. When you identify the 'I AM' with an object or a person whom you are attached to ("I am in love with her/him," "I am attached my possessions – to money, my car, my house; or attached to fame or power") you become overwhelmed with grief, sorrow and disappointment when that fame or power is lost, and when that object or person is separated from you. The identification with the personality is sustained by memory and desire, through its body and intellect. This attachment prevents you from knowing and abiding in your inner Self, the 'I Am Presence', the Divinity that is your true identity.

By removing the sense of identification of "me" and "mine", and "I am this or that", to the inner stillness of "I AM" (your true spiritual nature, the eternal blissful Self), you free yourself from attachment and suffering.

The moon reflects the light of the sun; similarly, the ego is a mere reflection of the Self (the I AM). If I declare: "I am Stephen," there is an immediate identification with my personality, the ego. If I simply say, "I AM," that is the God-Self, the Divinity within, my true spiritual identity or reality.

How to use Affirmations

The first step is to determine what kind of transformation you want to bring about in yourself – an intention or a goal. Or you can also determine what attitude, quality, value or characteristic you want to remind yourself of or develop in yourself. Select an affirmation that sincerely reflects best what you wish to achieve or transform in your life.

Remember, every thought you think and every word you express, whether it is negative or positive, is an affirmation that creates your life experience. So be aware of what you think and say so that you can direct your life in positive ways. Release your limitations and take control over your thinking by eliminating negative, complaining, and blaming affirming words and phrases such as – *"I can't" "I'll never be able to..." "It's too difficult for me" "I know it won't work" "It's impossible" "It's because of him/her that I'm unable to..." "I'm not good enough" "I don't deserve to have..."* – from your vocabulary. Replace such negative and limiting thoughts with positive thoughts that will empower you. Choose only those thoughts and words that will create *positive* results for you. Be careful in the way you word your affirmations, for example if you were to say, "I don't want to be unhealthy anymore," this is not an effective affirmation to be in good health. State clearly in the present tense what you *do* want. *"I choose to be healthy now."*

For affirmations to effectively help you, they need to be repeated consciously with awareness, with intensity of attention and with faith and conviction. Affirmations work well when there is *feeling* behind them. There is energy in emotion and feeling, and this energy activates thought into action. To make you feel empowered, choosing the right affirmation is important, particularly in how the words make you *feel*. For the affirmation you are repeating to be successful, you need to affirm things that you *believe* in and *motivate* you into action to make positive changes in your life. For example, if I affirm, "I am wealthy," while in the background of my thoughts I'm thinking that my bank account is overdrawn and I have no savings, I would not feel wealthy at all. But if the affirmation were changed to, *"I have the potential to be wealthy"* or *"I choose to be wealthy"* or *"I allow money to flow freely to and from me,"* that empowers me to believe that *I can* become wealthy by motivating myself to take action and changing the way I manage my finances.

If the affirmation you are using is having an opposite effect to how you feel and what you intended, and it just makes you feel worse, then change the wording by adjusting the statement and adding such words as: *"I choose to..." "I have the potential to..." "I am willing to..." "I am guided to..." "I trust..." "I allow..." "I can..."* to your affirmation. Do not allow doubt to dominate your feeling. Knowing that the Spirit of God within you is the true Source of your supply, *believe*, *trust* and have *faith* that your positive thoughts have divine power to attract to you what you need and when you need it. Know that your affirmation is true to your inner reality. Just keep your mind focused on the Presence within, and let the Divine Power work in and through you. Trust your intuition and be *willing* to change and take action, so that you can manifest your dreams and live the purposeful, healthy, abundant, peaceful, loving and joyful life you want to live.

Affirmations need to be phrased in the *present* tense as if the statement is already true, and repeated regularly throughout the day, for as many days or weeks until the desired result, change or awakening is attained. Affirm your positive statements always with gratitude, *"I am thankful for my life,"* for present blessings.

The best time to practise positive affirmations is immediately after awakening in the morning, or at night, just before going to sleep. Other good times are after deep meditation when the mind is calm and clear, and during relaxed periods throughout the day when your mind is calm and more receptive to positive suggestions. By allowing time to meditate before repeating your affirmations, your conscious mind will have calmed its constant stream of thoughts, allowing the message you are affirming to reach your subconscious, so that the seed of new belief can be implanted.

Affirmations can also be repeated throughout the day in your activities such as walking, travelling on public transport, or while you are in the bath or shower. Short affirmations of one or two sentences that are easily remembered are good for this, such as: *"In God's Presence I am guided and protected"* or *"I am joyful, peaceful and whole."* To emphasise the truths you want to live by, your positive affirmative statements can be spoken, thought, read or written.

Writing Affirmations

To add power and action to your positive affirmations, write them down on paper or in a notebook, or even use sticky Post-it notes on objects such as the bathroom mirror, fridge, cupboards or car dashboard. To impress the affirmation in your mind, write it in red ink.

Begin by choosing an intention that you would like to manifest in your life. Then writing your affirmation, choose only those words that are meaningful, and that awaken the desired sense of *feeling* that you desire to feel when your affirmation manifests.

So you can easily remember your affirmation and be able to repeat it frequently, keep it to one short positive sentence. For example: *"I am enfolded in God's ever-present love,"* or *"I am able to accomplish all that is mine to do,"* or *"I choose to live in higher awareness,"* or *"I am willing to open my mind and heart to all that is good," or "I forgive and release myself from negative energy."*

For the affirmation to be really effective make a resolve to repeat it daily for 21 days. The more you affirm something the more your mind will accept it, and the more positive changes you will experience as new opportunities and healthy behaviours to transform your life.

Method

1. Relax your body from tension, and release your mind from all anxiety, worry and restlessness. To relax your mind and body, inhale deeply, hold the breath, and tense all the muscles in your body. Hold both the breath and the tension in your muscles for a few seconds, then simultaneously release the breath and the tension and relax. Repeat the process of tensing and relaxing three times, then finish by completely relaxing, and *feel* the relaxation and the flow of energy into your body.
2. Sit still in a comfortable meditation posture with your head, neck and spine held straight in alignment. Close your eyes and become aware of your natural breath flowing in and out. Practise this breath awareness for a few minutes or until the mind becomes calm.
3. When your body is still and your mind is calm and free from restlessness, then repeat your affirmation with deep concentration; and with your eyes closed, looking inwardly bring your attention and awareness to the frontal part of your brain at the midpoint between the eyebrows (spiritual eye, the seat of spiritual consciousness). Repeat your affirmation several times aloud *verbally* to command the attention of your conscious mind. Then repeat it *quietly* to absorb the meaning more deeply. Continue to speak it very quietly, in

a *whisper*. Then repeat the affirmation *silently*, contemplating the meaning more intently as you gaze into your spiritual eye, raising your consciousness into the greater reality of superconsciousness; the divine guidance can work through you.

4. After the practice session maintain awareness and inner calm. Establish the feeling within you that the condition you desire is already a part of your life. Visualise and know this to be true. With inner conviction, know, feel and visualise that your affirmations are working for you now! **Remember:** An affirmation declares that which is true and opens the way for its manifestation. Affirmations gain their power from *repetition*. Through repeated affirmation you can strengthen and spiritualise your awareness of any quality you want to develop.
5. End your session by offering your affirmation with heartfelt love and attunement to the Divine with a prayer. Repeating your affirmation and prayer with deep attention and devotion spiritualises it, and changes it into superconscious experience.

Everyday Affirmations and prayers

You may wish to use the following affirmations and prayers that are paired together below, or you can create your own for various purposes.

Clearly define your plans and intentional actions. Use intention as a powerful tool to create the life of your highest good:

Affirmation

Aligning my desires and actions with
the power of the Divine Self within,
I confirm my commitment to right living and
spiritual practice with decisive actions.

Prayer

O Infinite Spirit within, lift up and expand my consciousness that I may see with new clarity and spiritual understanding. Aum, Peace, Amen.

Remain focused on your intentions without distraction and allow the results to unfold in divine order to create what you envision.

Affirmation

I release all thoughts of discord and align my thoughts and my life with divine order, as a pathway to releasing my inner potential and spiritual awakening.

Prayer

O Divine Self, inspire and guide my will and thoughts to express only that which is true and in divine order. Aum, Peace, Amen.

Firmly resolve to be completely spiritually awake and to remain faithful and loyal to a true, effective spiritual path that brings the lasting peace and love of spiritual fulfilment.

Affirmation

I choose to be firmly established in the awareness of my pure essence of Being and constantly aware of my divine relationship with the Infinite.

Prayer

O blessed Lord the Blissful Self within,
Teach me to live each moment in awareness
and appreciation for life, knowing that it is
your ever-Divine Presence expressing through me.
Aum, Peace, Amen.

Decide what is to be accomplished in your life. Acquire the necessary knowledge and skills to transform your life, then with firm resolve and conviction proceed until your innate divine qualities and knowledge of higher realities are fully Self-revealed.

Affirmation

Enfolded in unconditional divine love,
and guided by the indwelling Divine Presence,
I firmly resolve to live in the consciousness of the Divine,
the eternal Truth, knowing that I will be divinely supported
through every challenge toward Self- and God-realisation.

Prayer

O infinite Self, help me to awaken in the light of
that higher consciousness that knows no boundaries.
Aum, Peace, Amen.

Acknowledge your immortal essence of Being and open your mind to Infinite possibilities.

Affirmation

I am a divine Being of pure awareness; a sacred Being of Truth.
Peace, love, joy, power, wisdom and intelligence are all a part
of my spiritual nature. Unbounded by time, space or
circumstance, I am open to Infinite possibilities
to create a positive and fulfilling life.

Prayer

O blessed Lord, make me an instrument of Your Truth.
Fill me with Your Light. Teach me to see with the all-pervading
spiritual eye of wisdom, that I may always abide in the
ever-present Reality, of the Self within.
Aum, Peace, Amen.

The determined dedication of the heart, mind and will to God, the Supreme Divinity within you, is the means to complete fulfilment. As soon as your essential nature is known, all misconceptions about your identity as a separate and limited being are instantly dispelled.

Affirmation

I am distinct from the body, mind, ego, and intellect, which perform their activities due to the Light and Energy of the eternal blissful Self that I AM.

Prayer

Divine Spirit, may Your Divine grace keep me ever steadfast in the awareness of your loving Presence and everlasting Love.
Aum, Peace, Amen.

Focus on your strengths not your weaknesses, and exchange your self-limiting thoughts of limitation, lack and weakness for positive unlimited attitudes and thoughts of abundance, inner strength and courage to overcome all obstacles, difficulties and challenges in your life.

Affirmation

I abide in a consciousness of Truth and courage.
The Presence of God within me is my power and strength to overcome all difficulties and challenges. I can reach my goals and overcome any challenge.

Prayer

O Divine Lord, open my soul to unlimited good.
Open my mind and heart, and connect them to Your
Divine Source of power, wisdom, ideas and inspiration.

Know and realise that you are a divine Being; you are not the physical body or the mind. Release any erroneous beliefs about your physical health, for in truth you are more than your physical body. You are the divine life force within the body that is more potent than any imbalance or disease.

Affirmation

I am one with the perfect expression of Divine Life, flowing within every atom, cell, nerve, tissue, muscle, bone and organ of my body.
The healing power of Divine Life sustains my body,
and enlivens and restores me to wholeness now.

Prayer

O Divine Mother, enfold me in your perfect healing Light.
May your Radiant Light, omnipresent in my body,
cleanse and purify as it circulates and flows into every body cell.
Your unlimited Supreme Power brings radiant healing and
wholeness to every cell of my body.
Aum, Peace, Amen.

By letting go of limited thinking, negative influences and bad habits that drain your energy, you can empower yourself and open the way to receiving new blessings, freedom and contentment.

Affirmation

My trust is in the power of God within. I let go of all that
which no longer serves my highest good, and being
guided by the inner Light and Wisdom within
I embrace my inner transformation with joy!

Prayer

Heavenly Father, guide my life to unfold in harmony with Thine.
Free my mind from all negative influences, habits and beliefs
that do not serve my higher purpose.
As I let go of the erroneous ways that kept me in bondage,

and rest in Your inner calm and peace,
I am guided to my higher purpose.
Aum, Peace, Amen.

Good health is nurtured by right diet and lifestyle, which includes exercise, proper breathing, relaxation, sufficient sleep, prayer and positive thinking, affirmations, prayer and meditation.

Affirmation

God's perfect Love and healing Power fill my mind and body, sustaining my energy and wholeness in health and harmony.

Prayer

O Infinite Spirit, recharge and vitalise my mind and body with Thy all life-giving Energy. I attune myself to Your Divine wisdom to guide me in positive ways. Strengthen my willpower to overcome any thoughts of weakness, limitation or failure, for Your Power and Life Energy that flow within me are greater.
Aum, Peace, Amen.

Prayer and how to pray effectively

If we neglect prayer and if the branch is not connected to the vine, it will die. That connecting of the branch to the vine is prayer. If that connection is there then love is there, then joy is there, and we will be the sunshine of God's love, the hope of eternal happiness, the flame of burning love.
Mother Theresa (1910–1997), *Everything Starts from Prayer*, Ashland, Oregon: White Cloud Press, 1998

We are divine beings, and prayer and meditation are the surest ways to remember the presence of the Divine or God within you.

The process of prayer is another way of focusing the mind on the Divine. Through prayer the scattered rays of the mind concentrate upon the object of prayer. It helps you to turn your attention inward to connect consciously with the Divine, so that your thoughts, feelings, beliefs and attitudes are in harmony with the flow of the cosmic process. Prayer opens and enlarges the heart; it opens the door to deeper levels of consciousness, and to God's omnipresent grace.

More than merely an outer posture or position, true prayer is an inner attitude. When we pray in the silence of our hearts, with the heart's intention to feel the presence of God, we enter inner communion with the Divine, a presence, power and activity that helps us to release our outer concerns and open the door of our heart to God's love, wisdom and guidance. Prayer centred in the heart is a portal to accessing God available at any time.

Prayer may not always change the situation, but it changes your attitude toward the situation and gives you hope, which in turn can your life.

In Him we live and move and have our being.
Bible, Acts 17:28

To pray is an act of faith, it is the conviction that the Divine Presence or God is omnipresent, omnipotent and omniscient in everything, everywhere and in every moment – God alone *is*. Prayer is the conscious intention to experience the presence of God, seeking to recognise our awareness with God, and opening ourselves to God's omnipresent power that flows through us. When we pray in this way, we are not praying to God or for God, as something separate from us, but from that divine presence which is our essential Being or Self. Pray with the realisation that you are one with God, and God's Will is done in you. When you pray do not think of God as being outside of you, for God is *within* you in the Eternal Now, the prayer and the answer are as one. God the Ultimate Reality is always the only Life expressing in and through all. Your consciousness is the point through which God expresses Itself. And it is also through your consciousness that you express the living Presence of God the Christ within you.

Pray without Ceasing

> *Rejoice at all times. Pray without ceasing. Give thanks in everything, for this is the will of God in Christ Jesus for you.*
> Bible, Thessalonians 5:16–18

> *As oil poured from one vessel to another falls in an unbroken line, as chimes coming from a distance fall upon the ear as one continuous sound, so should the mind flow towards God in one continuous stream.*
> Swami Vivekananda (1863–1902), *Religion of Love*, published by Swami Bodhasarananda, Advaita Ashrama Mayavati, Champawat, Uttarakhand, Himalayas, 2012

The Apostle Paul maintained a sacred inner peace within, where God was a constant presence. To pray without ceasing is to live in the actual presence of God, and is a direct expression of love for the Divine. Prayer connects us consciously with God. By practising the presence of God at all times and in any place, every thought can be a prayer.

Prayer together with meditation becomes a way of life; they are essential to our life, to our very being. The truth of your divine nature is the most important thing you need to pray for and hold to without ceasing. The earnest, consistent and constant spiritual practice of prayer and meditation opens your conscious awareness to experience your eternal oneness with the infinite love and peace of the Divine. Divine love and everlasting joy are the essence of your being.

Devote yourselves to prayer, keeping alert in it with thanksgiving.
Bible, Colossians 4:2

Be Still and know that I am God

Be still and know that I am God.
Psalm 46:10

Following Prayer and meditation you focus your attention within and abiding in the inner Self, rest in the inner calmness and silence, in the stillness of the Divine, the nature of God, the Source of truth and life. As you tune into the Divine, all your restless thoughts become silent. You remain calm in harmony, peace, and true happiness, and experience a joy that is truly satisfying – you are in the kingdom of the Infinite.

God speaks in the silence of our heart, and when we listen. And then we speak to God from the fullness of our heart, and God listens.
Mother Theresa, *Everything Starts from Prayer*, page 80, Ashland, Oregon: White Cloud Press, 1998

After prayer and meditation and returning to your everyday activities, you practise the art of living by performing all your duties with acceptance in a calm and positive way without losing your inner peace and harmony. By remaining calm at all times and by keeping your faith strong in the Divine, realising that all that exists is centred in the Divine, you will have the inner power and strength to overcome all difficulties, trials and challenges, and you will always have mental peace.

A drop of ocean water

As a drop of ocean water that has been separated from its source eventually makes its way back to the mighty ocean, we are inevitably drawn back into the awareness of our oneness with God. The drop of water may evaporate high up into the clouds, then be blown by the wind, and fall as snow on a mountain. Eventually the snow will melt and the drop will become part of a small trickle of water, that flows into a brook, and into a stream, then into a river, until it finally returns to the sea and the ocean.

Like the drop of water that cannot be forever separated from its source: the ocean, so our prayers which are for the purpose of *knowing* God return us to the awareness of our oneness in God. When we connect with that divine energy that is God, we break out of our sense of separation and limitation, and experience our real unlimited nature.

Concept of God – Who or what do we pray to?

Prayer is allowing ourselves to enter into the Presence of the Divine Being, and that Presence is not sitting on a golden throne in some undefined quarter of a celestial heaven. If we think that, we have definitely got our geography wrong, and we become a religious tourist. Anyone who chooses to go to heaven out of fear of damnation in hell, thinking that God will sit on his throne and judge you, goes against all intelligent reason and experience of love of one who is truly spiritual. A belief that goes against reason and experience is an error. This concept of God which relies on a set of non-verifiable beliefs has been blindly accepted and definitely misunderstood! The old religious concept of an anthropomorphic God who rewards you in heaven if you give praise to him and punishes you if you do not needs to be dispensed with, for if God is a source of fear, he must be fallible. Beware of those theologies that programme you not to think, question or discern discriminately, but only want you to obey, with no possibility of change.

Before you pray it is meaningful to have an understanding of what God is; a concept of God which can be with form or without form. Remember that if God is omnipresent, omniscient and omnipotent, then God is all-pervasive in everything – space, time, galaxies, solar systems, the sun, stars, planets, minerals, plants, animals and humans. God is not separate from his creation. God is immanent, and ever-present as the innate Intelligence within creation, giving it life and activity. There is an all-knowing (known and unknown), all-powerful and intelligent force that is pervading. How can you know and experience God? **You can *know* what God is through *direct* experience in the stillness of deep meditation, in oneness with the Divine.** God or Divine Self is Ever-conscious, Ever-existing, Ever-new Bliss (*Sat-Cit-Ānanda*). That is where the Kingdom of God is, *within* you, always present here and now, not in the future.

In the formless aspect God, the Supreme Reality, which has the Divine aspects of infinite Love, Joy or Bliss, is Infinite, Omnipresent, so wherever you are God *is*. You can establish your connection with God in meditation and prayer by feeling God's formless Presence in any of God's qualities – love, peace, calmness, wisdom and joy – within you, as you pray *in* God.

How to Pray Effectively

Prayer is not asking. It is a longing of the soul. It is a daily admission of one's weakness. It is better in prayer to have a heart without words than words without a heart.

Mahatma Gandhi

If we really want to pray, we must first listen: for in the silence of the heart God speaks.
Mother Theresa, *Everything Starts from Prayer*, page 22, Ashland, Oregon: White Cloud Press, 1998

With closed eyes lift up your inner gaze not to the lofty skies or heaven, but to that higher consciousness located at the midpoint between the eyebrows, the centre of intuition and spiritual perception. Concentrate deeply there and transmit your soul prayer call from that centre of soul-intuition. When your mind is calm and still through deep meditation, pray for the awareness of God's Presence to be felt within you. In this Divine Presence and one power that is always within you and with you, and that can never be separate from you, there is no limitation, no time, and no space where God is not.

In meditative silence with your consciousness inwardly calm and focused, intuitively listen in your heart centre of consciousness – the receiver – to receive and hear God's silence. Enter an inner communion with the Divine, dissolving all sense of individuality and separation until you experience a oneness with that great Love, Bliss, Wisdom, Calmness, Peace, and Light of God. You can end your prayer for the well-being, happiness and peace of those close to you, your family and friends, and for world peace.

Fix a definite time every day for praying to God and let that period be dedicated to Him for the rest of your life.
Sri Anandamayi Ma

Pray from an awareness of the Divine Presence within you

The Divine Presence is with us all the time. We have but only to allow it to move within us. In the silence of our hearts the Divine speaks to our soul and listens to us.

So I tell you, whatever you ask for in prayer, believe that you

have received it, and it will be yours.
Mark 11:24

Seek first His kingdom and his righteousness and all these things will be given to you as well.
Matthew 6:33

In prayer you need not request anything at all, because we already have access to all that God is. Many times the things for which we pray are obstacles to our spiritual progress. It is best to pray for results which reduce your desires and promote peace, love, and understanding in you. Prayer changes things and circumstances; prayer without any material motive is a powerful means for attaining spiritual transformation and fulfilment.

We do not pray to God or for God, but from an *awareness* of the Divine presence within us. In prayer we can *affirm* what already exists in Truth. By praying affirmatively we assert that we are being guided to our highest good, irrespective of any outer circumstances or temporary appearances. Through affirmative prayer we faithfully pray, giving gratitude in advance that the Divine is blessing our lives with unlimited possibilities and meeting our needs. Below is the well known prayer associated with Saint Francis of Assisi (1182–1226AD): *"Make me an Instrument of Thy peace."* The prayer has been slightly adjusted to make it an 'affirmative prayer'.

Lord, I am an instrument of Your peace.
Where there is hatred I sow love;
where there is injury, pardon;
where there is doubt, faith;
where there is despair, hope;
and where there is sadness, joy.
O Heavenly Father, I do not so much seek
to be consoled as to console;
to be understood as to understand;

to be loved as to love.
For it is in giving that we receive;
it is in forgiving that we are forgiven;
and it is in dying to ego-consciousness
that we are born into eternal Divine Consciousness.

The best type of prayer is that which asks for the highest things: *awareness* and *Presence of the Divine*. The highest prayer of all is for the *love* of the Supreme Being, the Source of lasting happiness and true security. It is not praying *to* God, but praying *from* a consciousness of God, so that you become a radiating centre of God-consciousness and immersed in this energy, power, love and light to draw to you whatever you need for your health and well-being, abundance, prosperity and success here and now.

Prayer begins with words and thoughts but ends deep inside ourselves in silence, in absolute stillness in the presence of God. It is in this still silence that we find inner peace, contentment, strength, healing, and joy. *"Be still and know that 'I Am' God"* (Psalm 46:10). In other words: Be still and know your Self. In stillness, there is no movement because you are beyond space and time. The moment you are still, you will know the *'I Am'* within you; there is just the awareness of the oneness of Being. The Sanskrit mantra *So-ham*, which is the sound of the inhalation and the exhalation, is really an echo of *'I Am'*.

You can pray at any time and in any place, but it works particularly well when you meditate first and enter into the stillness of your heart, the realm of soul intuition within the essence of your being. It is in that inner silent peace and joy of deep meditation that you have made the Divine connection.

Every day, begin and end your meditation with a prayer. Sit quietly, and with a calm mind and an open heart, pray deeply in the spontaneous language of your heart with faith, love, and devotion – "Infinite Spirit, Heavenly Father, Divine Mother, Friend, Beloved God, bless me, guide me, and protect me, show me the true path to

Self-realisation." Pray using the words that come to you naturally and in the consciousness that the Divine is with you. Then in the inner silence of your Self, the Divine will communicate to you through the silence of intuition. Prayer begins with words, flows into a silent aspiration in the heart, and transforms itself naturally and spontaneously into meditation – the ultimate goal of prayer.

Prayer becomes effective only when it has the total support of your faith, a spirit of self-surrender of ego, devotion, and intense aspiration with divine will-force as a continual spiritual discipline. First you attain divine attunement with the Divine in the stillness of meditation, immersing yourself in calmness and inner peace. In this way, prayer detaches the will from desires and objects, and spiritually focuses the mind, lifting it upward to a higher reality.

Prayer blessing before meals

Food gives you life; it nourishes your mind and body. It contains the life and nourishment that the Divine and Nature gave it, but that life needs to be raised to a higher degree, and stimulated and enhanced by your blessings. Before you begin your meal, sit quietly in silence, and with gratitude obtain that life and nourishment that the Divine has placed in your food by first saying grace. A brief heartfelt prayer such as:

Receive Lord in Thy Light, the food we eat, for it is Thine.
Infuse it with Thy love, Thy energy, Thy life Divine. Aum, Amen.

Sanskrit Prayers

The following Sanskrit prayers are traditionally used in India, and are commonly chanted before or after meditation.

Sarveśām svastir bhavatu
Sarveśām shāntir bhavatu
Sarveśām pūrnam bhavatu
Sarveśām mangalam bhavatu

Oṁ śhānti, śhānti, śhānti.

May there be happiness for all
May there be peace for all
May there be completeness in all
May there be success for all
Om peace, peace, peace.

Oṁ, Sarve Bhavantu sukhinah
Sarve santu nirāmayāh
Sarve bhadrani paśyantu
Mā kashchit dukha bhāgbhavet
Oṁ śhānti, śhānti, śhānti.

May all be prosperous and happy
May all be free from disease
May all see what is spiritually uplifting
May no one suffer
Om peace, peace, peace.

Asato mā sadgamaya
Tamaso mā jyotir-gamaya
Mrityor-mā āmritam gamaya
Oṁ śhānti, śhānti, śhānti.

From ignorance, lead me to truth;
From darkness, lead me to light;
From death, lead me to immortality
Aum peace, peace, peace.

Grace of God

For in Him (God) we live and move and have our being.
Acts 17:28

Grace is the unconditional love for us, that accepts us exactly as we are. In the New Testament of the Bible the Greek translation of the word 'Grace' is *charis* meaning blessing, favour or kindness.

Grace is the ever-present, all-pervasive divine energy that connects you to the ultimate Truth, to the source of your Being. Grace is the highest gift from the Divine, and it can be accessed anywhere and at any time. Grace is seeking to know itself through the perfection of your own life. Just as water pervades the waves, oceans and seas, streams, rivers and lakes, so grace is always present in your life whether you know it or not. You are here in the physical body, in this world, because of divine Grace.

> *The winds of grace are always blowing, but it is you who must raise your sails.*
> Rabindranath Tagore

Grace can manifest in many ways and the result can appear in any form. It can manifest as wisdom, inspiration, material aid, and give protection from accidents and disasters. The greatest grace is that which makes you virtuous and selflessly loving. Not even the desire to realise Divinity can be obtained without God's Grace. The means, the ability, and your achievement of the goal are all dependent upon God's grace.

Divine Grace is like sunlight shining on all. God's benevolence and unconditional love blesses us regardless of whether we are deserving or the least deserving, merited or unmerited. It is our birthright to receive God's blessings, love and light. Each of us has been endowed with divine consciousness, free will, and the grace to respond to God.

Grace is available to you in every moment

Grace is available to you in every moment, but it needs your free will to choose to accept it and to be open to it, and your inner attunement to respond to it, so that it may fill your consciousness and dissolve all that resists it. Then the Divine can unfold within you and free you from limitation, bondage, suffering and separation.

Grace is God's gift of unconditional love and mercy that is given freely to us, and we have been given free will, to act according to our own will, to choose acceptance or refusal of it. Through sincere and earnest devoted spiritual practice (*sādhanā*) – meditation and prayer – you open the door of your heart so the sunlight of grace may illumine it. Then the divine grace and energy flows naturally to those who love and serve others unconditionally.

For those who are awakening on the spiritual path, individual effort and divine grace are both interdependent. To call or pray for God's grace you must first use all your own abilities and own best effort to help yourself.

Grace may not necessarily remove all your physical suffering and sorrows, but if you have the divine grace you can pass through the challenges and ordeals of life more successfully than if you did not have it. Grace gives you inner strength and courage to face all difficulties and challenges in life, and enables you to feel the divine Presence working in you and through you, bringing the blessed gift of inner peace to remain inwardly calm. When you are aware of grace working in your life, your whole life will flow and be blessed with grace.

Earning Grace

What is unique to the human being is that it has the capacity to choose. It is freedom of will or free will, which if not used in the right way can cause pain and suffering and be a bondage to us. Our likes and dislikes (*rāga-dveṣa*) can cause problems in using our free will. Even to a simple act of giving that does not come from your heart – your giving may be resentful, you feel pressured to give some money to a poor beggar on the street, and so to relieve you of the feeling of guilt for not giving, you indifferently drop some coins in his hat. This is not giving. It is only giving when it comes unconditionally from your heart; only then is it grace.

Tuning in to divine Grace

To get the right channel on a radio you need to tune the radio dial to connect to the correct station. Similarly, by intentionally tuning your mind in meditation and prayer you can connect to grace and Presence of the Divine. The more you pray, the more you align your mind – thoughts, feelings, attitudes and beliefs – in harmony with the grace of God, and you realise that you live by divine grace.

Sit steadily and calmly in the stillness of your meditation and with devotion invoke God's grace by prayer. Purity is a condition for receiving divine grace, so pray with a pure mind and an open heart:

> *May divine grace bless my meditation with love and devotion. May divine grace fill my mind and heart with truth. May I always be aware of the power of Your presence in my life, for it is being in attunement with You that I will find the solutions to all my problems, Amen.*

When your mind has been purified by prayer and meditation, it will direct you from within.

God's grace is abundant

God's grace is abundant, and provides and sustains the universe. In Jesus' positive words when he gave the Sermon of the Mount, he assures us of God's benevolent grace:

> *But seek first His kingdom* (within you) *and His righteousness, and all these things will be given to you as well. Therefore do not worry about tomorrow, for tomorrow will worry about itself.*
> Matthew 6:33–34

> *Ask and it will be given to you; seek and you will find; knock and the door will be opened to you.*
> Matthew 7:7

The Guru's grace

Besides God's grace there is also guru's grace (*guru-kṛpā*). The guru, who in his true nature is a divine manifestation of God, is a channel for the flow of divine grace. In human form the guru removes the veil of ignorance and reminds us of our real nature, our divine essence, and shows us the way to the Divine. We are all perfect by nature, but we have forgotten our eternal perfection, and so we continue to commit endless mistakes. The guru removes the darkness of ignorance and illumines our mind with spiritual light.

The greatest guru is the *Avatāra*, the Divine Incarnation, who is able to bring illumination to thousands of people. The great *Kriya Yoga* lineage of the four great *Kriya Yogis*: Mahavatar Babaji, Lahiri Mahasaya, Swami Sri Yukteswar and Paramhansa Yogananda are all *Avatāras*. Jesus Christ is also a great *Avatāra*, who had the power to bring divine Light and illumine his disciples with spiritual consciousness, to transform the impure and to heal the sick.

The real guru who reveals to you the Truth is in your very own heart, is the point of contact with the Divine in yourself, the inner Teacher, that is always present within you. Hold on to your centre of consciousness but do not forget the infinite Consciousness that extends all around it.

To sail across the ocean of this life, unfurl your sails of love and devotion for the Divine; then you will catch more of the breeze of divine grace that is ceaselessly blowing, and it will take you forward even in the midst of shattering storms and trials of the world.

When you are aware of divine grace bestowed upon you, make good use of it to maintain the flow of your spiritual stream. With faith, willingness, and self-disciplined effort plus divine grace, you will be able to overcome all obstacles that come your way, and by conquering them, you will gain great strength of mind. The more your inner life is pure and strong, the more you will be in the flow of grace. The inner guru will direct you and will continue to help you until your spiritual goal is reached or attained.

Set the intention and resolve to meditate

To attain success in meditation you will need to cultivate dispassion and a strong aspiration or intense longing for Self-realisation. There are no short cuts or instant success in meditation; it cannot be attained in a short while, it is a long and gradual process. It takes years of patient and steadfast effort to change the quality of the mind. A mind that has been conditioned through habit to seek enjoyment, pleasure and happiness outwardly for many years and even lifetimes cannot be controlled, transcended and made pure overnight.

After setting the intention and making a resolve and commitment to meditating daily, you will then need to make a great effort to persevere with patience and vigilance over a long period of time.

To be successful in your spiritual practices and attain the greatest benefits from *Raja Yoga* and *Kriya Yoga* meditation, first set the intention to *want* to know the Absolute Truth, the Ultimate Reality. Whether we call the goal we are trying to reach *Truth*, *Ultimate Reality*, *Absolute*, *Brahman*, *Ātmān*, *Puruṣa*, *Divine Self* or *God*, know that it is the realisation of that highest and One Truth which liberates us from all illusion, ignorance, pain and suffering. Meditation is the key to unlock the secrets of life: it opens the doors of intuitive knowledge and leads us into realms of eternal Joy.

Decide now and positively resolve to make daily meditation become part of your everyday life. Affirm that you will meditate on a regular daily basis with a clear sense of purpose for living, and for realising your true spiritual divine nature: for becoming established in the awareness of your innermost Self, that is temporarily concealed, wrapped in the gross and subtle garments of the physical, astral and causal bodies.

Regular daily practice

Begin the habit of sitting for meditation at the same time, in the same place, and for the full length of time that you have set for yourself every day. Once you have developed this habit it will become easier to meditate. Then when you start to feel and experience the benefits of meditation – calmness, stillness, inner peace, inner joy, contentment, and feeling the energy – you will realise that meditation is actually your natural state of *Being*.

By practising regularly every day, you will reap the benefits that come from your sustained effort over a long period of time. When you establish stability in your meditation, you will create more freedom, balance, harmony, inner peace and joy in your life.

Train and discipline your mind to always put meditation first by keeping it at the top of the list of your daily priorities, and remember to always practise with enthusiasm and joy! Meditation must never become a dull routine, with the thought that joy and freedom are distant goals that you are trying to achieve. Your true eternal nature is Joy or Bliss (*Ānanda*). So, always enter your meditation with the feeling that you are already free and are joy itself. Always remember, you are *Sat-Cit-Ānanda* (ever-existent, ever-conscious, ever-new Joy).

When to meditate

You can meditate at any time or when it is convenient, but the most powerful times to meditate are at 6:00am (sunrise), 12:00 noon, 6:00pm (sunset) and 12:00 midnight. It is at these times that the gravitational pull of the sun works in harmony with the natural polarity of the human body.

In India, the yogis say that the most auspicious and peaceful time to meditate in the morning is between the early hours of 4:00am and 6:00am. This auspicious time is called *Brahmamuhurta*. At this time there is the quality of peacefulness and goodness (*sattva*) predominant in the mind of the meditator and in the atmosphere. There is a natural peace and stillness in the atmosphere at this time which makes it particularly favourable for meditating. It is also at this time and at dusk that the energy in the *suṣumnā nāḍī* (main subtle energy channel) flows readily. You will know when the *suṣumnā nāḍī* is flowing, because your breath will be flowing equally through both nostrils. This is when the *prāṇa* is naturally balanced between the *iḍā* and *piṅgala nāḍīs*. Like the coastal tides, *prāṇa* flows back and forth, or rotates between predominance in the *iḍā* and *piṅgala nāḍīs*. During the daytime *prāṇa* is more active in *piṅgala nāḍī*, causing your consciousness to become more active and extroverted. While at night, *prāṇa* shifts to being more predominant in the *iḍā nāḍī*, causing you to become more introverted.

If you want to meditate early in the morning, then make sure you go to bed early enough. For example, if you are going to get up at 6am, you will probably need at least six or seven hours sleep to feel refreshed. So, you would need to be in bed by 10 or 11pm. According to *Ayurvedic* philosophy *pitta* is most active in the middle of both the day and the night, so if you stay awake after 10pm you will find it difficult to get to sleep properly as the vital force – *pitta* ('to heat') – has a fiery active nature. If you wish to live a healthy and balanced life then you will need to synchronise yourself actively with nature's rhythms.

Also, eat lightly at night. If you go to bed with a heavy meal in your stomach it will disturb your sleep, and you may not be able to get up early.

As you approach your evening meditation time and afterwards sleep, you need to prepare by relaxing your body, mind and nervous system. For the mind to be serene you should avoid reading the newspapers and watching television, as any stimulating or disturbing news or programmes may disturb or agitate your mind, causing you to become tense, restless or anxious. To keep your mind serene, be selective in what you watch, hear and read, and avoid arguments, heated debates and excessive talking, so that you may have a sound and restful sleep and rise refreshed early for meditation.

As soon as you awake at 6am, get up immediately with the thought that you have an appointment with the Divine, and that you are now going to meditate. You need to be careful that you do not procrastinate by allowing yourself to roll over and full asleep again.

Length of meditation

If you are new to meditation, then sit for only 15 minutes in the beginning. It is more important to develop the constant habit of meditating regularly with alert attention than to sit for an hour feeling bored and restless, or to sit for half an hour one day and not meditate for the next few days.

Be consistent and regular in your practice. Begin with a daily 15-minute period of sitting for meditation, and try to sit for this period once in the morning and once in the evening, so that you have two meditations each day. If you can do this without creating any mental tension and can remain calmly centred without moving your body, then increase the length of your meditation to 20 minutes, and practise once or twice a day. As you progress, and find it more comfortable and relaxed to sit, then you can gradually increase the amount of time you sit for your meditation. Longer meditations, practised with deep focus and devotion, will help you to meditate more deeply. Usually it takes at least 45 minutes to one hour to go deep in meditation.

Where to meditate

For your daily sitting meditation, it is important to choose a private place, where you will not be disturbed, and which you will use regularly, and *only* for meditation. This will help to create a meditative vibration and a spiritual atmosphere in the place where you will sit. The place should be clean, comfortable, quiet, and peaceful, with natural air-ventilation. Ideally, have a separate room in your home for meditation; otherwise you can use a corner or smaller space within a room. In this space, place a small cupboard or small table to make an altar with, and place on it candles, incense, sacred pictures of your guru, saints or deity, and fresh flowers as an inspirational focus. To keep the spiritual energy and vibrations of this sacred space pure do not allow anyone to eat, drink, smoke, sleep or socialise there.

If you can, try to have your altar positioned so that it faces east or north. This is because the polarity of the magnetic fields of the Earth subtly influences us. Facing east or north will create a positive effect, while facing south will create a negative effect on the mind.

How to sit for meditation

Sitting for meditation or for *prāṇāyāma* requires a stable posture that is relaxed and comfortable. A posture in which you can maintain the natural curves of the spine, and remain seated in for a significant amount of time without any movement. When the body posture is held without effort, the breath is steady, quiet and subtle, and the mind is perfectly calm, you will be able to enter a deep state of stillness.

When sitting for meditation or for practising *prāṇāyāma*, it is necessary and important to sit with the upper body straight. To sit steadily and comfortably for any length of time the head, neck, spine and pelvis must be in alignment directly over the base of the spine. The neck, shoulders, back muscles, hips, knees and legs need to be relaxed. To maintain the natural curve of the lumbar spine, you need to sit up on the front of your sitting bones, not slumping back or arching forward. To sit in a cross-legged posture on a cushion or folded blankets, you need to sit high enough so that your knees are lower than your hips. This creates space in the front of the groin, making it easier for the pelvis to tilt into proper alignment.

A balanced spine supports the relaxation of the whole nervous system. If there are any imbalances and misalignments of these body structures, they will create discomfort, tension and pain. These imbalances can also impede or block the natural flow of *prāṇic* energy in the *suṣumnā nāḍī*.

Regular practice of Yoga postures will help enormously to improve alignment and comfort in the sitting poses by developing flexibility in the legs, hips, knees and spine. The Yoga postures will also help in strengthening the lower back and opening the chest, and developing and maximising your breathing.

Apart from *Vīrāsana* and *Vajrāsana*, all the other sitting poses listed below are cross-legged poses. These have the advantage of drawing the energy inwards toward the body and directing it upwards in the spine. It is also easier to apply *bandhas* (locks) in the cross-legged poses.

There are seven classical Yoga sitting postures (*āsanas*) for meditation:

1. ***Sukhāsana*** – Comfortable or easy pose (cross-legged)
2. ***Siddhāsana*** – Adept pose
3. ***Svastikāsana*** – Auspicious pose
4. ***Vīrāsana*** – Hero pose
5. ***Vajrāsana*** – Diamond pose or Thunderbolt pose
6. ***Ardha Padmāsana*** – Half-Lotus pose
7. ***Padmāsana*** – Lotus pose

Sukhāsana (Easy Pose)

For those who have difficulty in sitting for long periods in *Siddhāsana*, *Vajrāsana*, *Ardha Padmāsana or Padmāsana*, you can sit in *Sukhāsana* (easy pose). This is simply sitting cross-legged.

Sit on a firm cushion at an appropriate height for you to make the posture comfortable. Sitting on a firm cushion helps in stimulating and directing subtle energies. To avoid straining the back muscles try to keep the knees lower than the level of the hips, or at least at the same level. This allows your thighs to relax downward, reducing tension in the hips, and frees the spine to lengthen upwards. If you have a knee injury then support both knees with firm cushions, bolsters, or rolled blankets under them.

Cross both legs and place the right foot under the left thigh and the left foot under, or in front of, the right calf on the floor. If it is more comfortable, cross the legs in the opposite way. Sit upright with the weight of your body toward the forward edges of your sitting bones. Align the upper body and shoulders directly over the base of the spine. Lengthen the spine and open the chest, and draw your shoulders back. Place your hands relaxed palms upward in *Chin Mudrā* on your knees or thighs.

Sitting on a chair

If you are unable to sit comfortably and painlessly in *Sukhāsana*

(easy pose) then sit on an upright chair that has no armrests. (If your feet do not touch the floor, then support them with folded blankets.) The most important points are that the body is straight and in alignment, with the natural curves of the spine supporting the actions of the body; that the body is comfortable, relaxed; and that the body can remain still throughout the duration of the meditation or *prāṇāyāma* practice.

When sitting on a chair for meditation, sit with your back away from the back of the chair. Sit on the forward edge of the chair, with the soles of your feet flat on the ground and your spine upright. Gently round and arch the lower back a few times, tilting the pelvis forward and back, until you have centred your spine and sitting bones. When you feel your head, neck, spine and pelvis are aligned, then slightly lower your chin and lift the back of the skull to create space at the base of the occiput, where the head meets the neck.

For your comfort, make sure the chair is padded, or place a small cushion or folded blanket on it. Place the feet hip width apart on the floor, with the lower legs perpendicular to the floor. You may find it useful to have your hips slightly higher than the knees, so that the thighs slope slightly downward to minimise strain in the legs. A cushion can be used to raise the height of the seat if necessary. If you wish, you may place a woollen or silk cloth over your chair and extend it on to the floor for your feet to rest on. According to the yogis, wool and silk insulate against the subtle magnetic currents in the earth, which tend to pull the energy down.

Place the hands relaxed, palm upwards, at the junction of the thighs and abdomen (palms turned down you feel more grounded; palms turned up you feel more energised). Lift your shoulders, roll them up and back, and then drop and relax them. Keep the chest up. Lift up through your spine to the top of the head, so that your head, neck and spine are aligned straight, so that there is no impediment to the flow of subtle energy ascending in the spine to the higher brain centres.

Sitting on a meditation bench

Another useful prop for easy sitting is to use a wooden meditation bench with a slanting seat that allows the pelvis to tilt forward, and provides support and lift to the spinal column. The meditation bench stands approximately eight inches high from the floor, and is padded for comfort, or a small cushion is placed on it.

To sit on the meditation bench you need to go into a kneeling position with the buttocks sitting on the bench and folding your legs underneath with your shins resting on the floor. Keep the thighs parallel and straight out from the hips. Place the hands relaxed on the upper thighs, and keep the head, neck and spine aligned straight.

The sitting postures for the adept

For those of you who have more flexibility and suppleness in your body, and are not suffering from knee injuries, sit in any of the following postures: *Siddhāsana*, *Vajrāsana*, *Virāsana*, *Ardha Padmāsana* or *Padmāsana.* These postures present a greater challenge to your hips, knees and ankles.

Siddhāsana (Adept Pose; Perfect Pose)

Siddhā means 'perfected', 'accomplished'. A *Siddhā yogi* is one who is perfected or accomplished in Yoga, or adept (skilful) in Yoga. *Siddhāsana* is considered as the foremost meditation posture and a favourite of adept yogis.

Sit on the edge of a firm cushion or a folded blanket. Bend your right leg and place the sole of the foot flat against the inner left thigh with your heel pressing against the perineum (the area midway between the genitals and the anus), sitting on top of the right heel. Then bend your left leg and place the left ankle directly over the right ankle so that the ankle bones are touching and the heels are positioned one above the other. Press the pubis with your left heel directly above the genitals. Push the outer edge of the left foot and the toes between the right calf and thigh muscles. Grasp the right toes and pull them up in between the left calf and thigh.

In men, the base of the penis rests against the bottom heel. Lift the penis, scrotum, and testes up and out of the way, and then place the left heel close to the pubic bone.

Sit with the head, neck and spine in straight alignment, and with the knees touching the floor. Close the eyes, and place your hands on your knees or thighs with the palms either downward in *jñana mudrā* (gesture of intuitive knowledge) or palms upward in *chin mudrā* (gesture of consciousness). In both *mudrās* the tip of the index finger and thumb touch. The other three fingers are extended and relaxed.

Chin mudrā represents the union of the cosmic with the individual consciousness. The index finger represents individual consciousness and the thumb, cosmic consciousness. The three remaining fingers symbolise the three *Guṇas* (*Sattva*, *Rajas* and *Tamas*), the three fundamental qualities of Material Nature (*Prakṛiti*). The goal of the yogi is to transcend the three *Guṇas* and to unite with the Cosmic Self.

Both *mudrās* help to activate the lower lungs and encourage diaphragmatic breathing, and stimulate the grounding effects of *Apāna Vāyu* (functions in the region of the navel to the feet). *Chin mudrā* also stimulates *Prāṇa Vāyu*.

In this pose, the pressure of the heel against the perineum stimulates *mūlabandha,* and the pressure against the pubic bone stimulates the *svādhiṣṭhāna*, directing the *prāṇic* flow of energy from the lower *chakras* upward through the spine, stimulating the brain and calming the entire nervous system.

Note: Women, like men, should position the heel against the inner surface of the inferior pubic rami. But this means that the heel will have to be placed directly against the soft tissues of the genitals, well in front of the fourchette (the fold of skin which forms the union of the lower ends of the labia minora). The heel will be more intrusive in the female because the upside-down V formed by the pubic rami is shallower than in the male. If women sit directly on the floor without a cushion, the back of the lower heel will be in the exact place where both the urogenital and pelvic diaphragms are interrupted by the vaginal introitus.

The posture used by women is called ***Siddha Yoni āsana***. Sit with the legs straight in front. Bend your right leg and place the sole of the foot flat against the inner left thigh. Place the heel of the right foot firmly against or inside the labia majora of the vagina. Bend the left leg and position the left heel directly on top of the right heel so it presses the clitoris, and tuck the left toes down between the calf and thigh. Hold the toes of the right foot and pull them up between the left calf and thigh. The knees should be firmly on the floor, and the head, neck, and spine aligned straight. The hands are placed on the knees in either *jñana mudrā* or *chin mudrā*.

Benefits: Channels and directs the *prāṇic* life-energy to the *ājñā chakra*. Controls the nervous and *prāṇic* energy from *mūladhāra* and *svādhiṣṭhāna chakras*. Prevents blood pressure from falling too low during meditation, and helps to maintain the inner body temperature. It also stabilises the cardiac function. The two lower chakras: *mūladhāra* and *svādhiṣṭhāna* are stabilised and the *prāṇa* is redirected upward toward the higher *chakras*.

Svastikāsana (Auspicious Pose)

The symbol of the *svastika* represents the different corners of the earth and universe, the spokes, and their meeting point and centre of consciousness. *Svastikāsana* is the third most important classical meditation posture, after *Siddhāsana* and *Padmāsana*. The

Auspicious pose (*Svastikāsana*) does not involve as much strain on the leg joints; it can be managed for a long period of sitting.

Sit on the edge of a firm cushion or two folded blankets with the legs stretched forward. Bend the left leg and place the sole of your left foot against the right inner thigh. Take your right foot by the ankle and place it on top of your left calf, and position the outer edge of the foot and the toes in between the thigh and calf muscles. Place your hands relaxed on the knees with the thumb and index fingers touching, positioned in either *jñana mudrā* or *chin mudrā*. Keep the head, neck and spine in straight alignment.

The difference between this pose and *Siddhāsana* is that in *Svastikāsana* the heels are not in line with each other. This makes it slightly easier as it requires less hip flexibility than *Siddhāsana*. In *Siddhāsana* and *Svastikāsana*, both knees come close to the floor. This supports the lower back by creating a natural inward tilt to the sacrum, giving a slight arch to the lower back.

Svastikāsana activates and rejuvenates the entire nervous system.

Virāsana (Hero Pose)

For this sitting pose you will need one or two brick-shaped rubber blocks or folded blankets for a sitting support. Kneel on the floor with your knees about 4 inches (10 cm) apart with your feet separated slightly wider than your hips. The tops of the feet rest on the floor pointing straight back. Position the support block(s) between your feet with the long side of the block placed horizontally between your ankles. Make sure that both of your sitting bones are resting, and balanced evenly on the block, and comfortably supported.

If you are comfortable sitting on your heels without the block, then lift up enough to allow you to use your hands to pull your outer calf muscles away from the thighs before you sit down between your heels.

Place the hands palms down on your thighs close to the

abdomen. To come out of the pose, lean forward on to your hands and slowly straighten the knees, walk back and stand up.

Caution: *Virāsana* puts a slight twist in the knees, so if you have a knee injury be careful, and practise with awareness only under the competent guidance of an experienced teacher.

Vajrāsana (Diamond or Thunderbolt pose)

This pose is also used by Muslims and Zen Buddhists as a position for prayer and meditation.

Come up on to the knees (knee stand). Place the legs together, tilt the upper body forward and sit back by lowering the buttocks onto the inside surface of the feet with the heels touching the sides of the hips. Cross the right big toe over the left, or alternatively have the big toes touching each other.

Keep the trunk upright and place the hands together, palms up and relaxed, on the thighs. The head, neck and back should be upright and relaxed.

Ardha Padmāsana (Half-Lotus Pose)

This posture is recommended for those unable to sit comfortably in the Full Lotus pose (*Padmāsana*).

Sit on the edge of a firm cushion or two folded blankets with the legs stretched forward. Bend the right leg and place the foot very close to the body on the floor. Then bend the left leg and bring the foot very close to the body on top of the right thigh. Keep the head, neck and spine in straight alignment, and both knees resting on the floor.

Ardha Padmāsana can also be practised by bending the left leg first and bringing the right foot on top of the left thigh. To prevent imbalances in the hips and pelvis it is good to regularly change the crossing of the legs, so that both hips remain equally open. This principle also applies to the other crossed-legged postures.

Padmāsana (Full Lotus Pose)

Padmāsana is the Classic Yoga sitting pose for meditation that has a balancing influence on all the *chakras*. In pictures we see the great yogi-masters like Mahavatar Babaji, Lahiri Mahasaya, Swami Sri Yukteswar and Paramhansa Yogananda sitting in the superconsciousness state of *samādhi*, while sitting in the Full Lotus pose. But for most Westerners it is one of the most challenging poses to perform and so it is not practical as a meditation pose. It places stress on the knees and hip joints; it demands a very strong external rotation of the thigh bones in the hip sockets, and if the hip joints are tight, this pose can place enormous stress on the knees. The knee is a hinge joint with a limited capacity to rotate, and it is usually the intra-articular structures of the knee such as the cruciate ligaments and menisci ligaments (act as pads for the knee joint) that get torn in an injury.

It is essential first to be able to perform a full range of motion of the ball and socket hip joint to protect the hinge knee joint. So, unless you have practised it in your childhood and youth, it is not likely to work satisfactorily. But for those adepts who have mastered this beautiful looking pose, it is said to bring an incomparable feeling of repose and calmness to the mind.

If you are going to practise *Padmāsana* do not force yourself into it, but carefully learn progressively with appropriate warm-up stretches and modifications under the guidance of an experienced teacher who is able to practise it competently and safely. Avoid this pose if you have knee problems or varicose veins.

If *Padmāsana* or the 'Lotus Pose' can be practised properly and correctly, and one is able to sit in it comfortably, it gives great stability and strength to the lower back while locking the legs securely in place. It is difficult to fall over even if you were to fall asleep, this is why it is the chosen pose by *yogis* for going into the superconsciousness state of *samādhi*.

Benefits: *Padmāsana* purifies all the systems of the body, and brings calmness and joy to the yogi. It increases *sattva guṇa* (purity).

Warm-ups for lotus pose

A good practice before any exercise where the knees are to be rotated into advanced sitting poses, such as *Padmāsana*, is to take time to warm and relax them by rubbing the sides of both knees vigorously with the palms of your hands. Rub vigorously using a rotating motion. This allows the bursae located around the joint (functions to cushion the knee) to lubricate, protecting the knees from sudden forcible flexion. The aim of Lotus warm-ups is to increase movement in the hip and knee joints, and stretch the thigh muscles. Therefore, exercises where you work both inward and outward rotation are helpful in augmenting the multidirectional range of motion in the hips.

When you come out of *Padmāsana*, straighten the leg, raise the kneecap, and pull the toes toward the body, so as to elongate the hamstring and relieve any cramps in the muscles.

First warm-up – Half Butterfly Pose

Sit with your back and legs straight. Breathing normally, place the right foot with the sole of the foot facing upward, on top of the left thigh as close to the hip as possible. *(If this leg position is difficult then place the foot on the floor alongside the inside of the thigh close to the body.)*

Hold the toes of the right foot with the left hand, and with slight pressure move your knee up and down ten times with the right hand.

Return to the starting position and perform the exercise with the left leg.

Benefits: Stretches the muscles of the inner hip and thighs, and encourages blood circulation into the hips.

Second warm-up – Full Butterfly Pose

Resting firmly on your sitting bones, sit on a cushion on the floor. Bring the soles of the feet together and draw the heels close into the groin. Clasp the feet with interlocked fingers and pull against the feet for leverage. Open the knees and press them toward the floor.

Inhale, lift the lower back, and extending the sternum, elongate the spine to the crown of the head. Exhale, creating a shoulder-blade squeeze, and slightly arch the lower spine, and work to lower the thighs toward the floor.

Third warm-up – The Cradle Pose

From the same sitting position as before, outstretch your right leg. Take hold of the left leg, and keeping the left foot up high, place it into the crook of the right arm at the elbow. Bring the left arm around and interlock the hands, creating your cradle (like holding a baby). Inhale, elongate and straighten the spine by extending the sternum upward. Exhale as you rock the cradled leg from right to left.

Inhale, elongating the spine again. Exhale, this time hugging the leg closer to your chest. Hold the position and feel the stretch in the thigh. Repeat the process with the other leg.

Full Lotus Pose *(Padmāsana)*

Sit with the legs extended straight in front of you. Then, slowly and carefully bend your left leg, holding the left foot with your hands. Turn the foot around so that the sole is facing you. Place the instep up high on the thigh as you lower the knee to the floor. The heel should be close to the pubic bone.

Bend the right leg. Holding the right foot with your hands, place the instep up high on the left thigh.

In the final position, both knees should ideally touch the floor. The head, neck and spine must be aligned with the shoulders relaxed, and the hands relaxed on the knees in either *jñana mudrā* or *chin mudrā*. Close the eyes and relax the whole body

A comfortable alternative to the Lotus pose

Padmāsana is an excellent posture for stability – it locks the pelvis into a perfect vertical position, keeping the spine upright and aligned. The pelvis is moved into the vertical position by the pulling of the gluteus medius muscles. The sitting bones are positioned correctly and the knees are rooted firmly to the floor.

For many Yoga practitioners, the Lotus pose (*Padmāsana*) is extremely difficult to accomplish, because in order for the feet to rest high on the thighs without injuring the knees, the thighs have to rotate outward about 116 degrees in the hip sockets, and the knees have to move closer together. There is also a considerable amount of strain on the knee joints; forcing oneself into this pose can easily injure a knee by tearing the meniscus ligament. But there is an alternative substitute – a comfortable, steady, supported version that combines the balance between the stability of *Padmāsana* (lotus pose) and the ease and comfort of *Sukhāsana* (easy pose) to create stability, comfort and ease.

Preparation:

1. To begin your practice you will need to sit against a wall on a carpeted floor to cushion your ankles (or you can fold a yoga mat). You will also need three or four folded blankets to sit on and another blanket rolled into a long roll to place over your feet. Place the three or four folded blankets parallel against the wall.

Technique:

2. Sit on the folded blankets with your back upright against the support of the wall. Then cross your legs and bring the right leg in so that your shins contact each other, and each foot rests on the floor under the opposite thigh.
3. Adjust the height of the knees until they are parallel to the floor.
4. Place the long rolled blanket over the tops of both feet and adjust it to support the legs.
5. Tilt your pelvis forward by leaning your upper body forward, then sit upright with your back against the wall. Rest the backs of your hands on your thighs, so that the hands are relaxed.
6. Roll the tops of your shoulders back and lean your head gently against the wall.
7. With the head, neck and spine in alignment, keep the chest lifted and relax your abdomen and diaphragm muscle as you breathe slowly and rhythmically.

Concentration: Focusing the mind

Focusing the mind means *concentration*, not allowing your mind to get scattered in all directions, but holding it to one point of focus. This is like a magnifying glass that concentrates the light rays of the sun into one powerful beam of energy strong enough to burn a piece of paper. All the different rays of the mind's attention have to be brought together and made one-pointed by focusing on one thing.

The more your mind's attention is scattered, the more you become involved with your senses and desires, leading to restlessness. If your mind is restless, continually moving in the turbulent realm of the sense world, the less consciousness you have of your true nature, and knowledge of Supreme Consciousness.

Meditation is like a bird: it needs two equally strong wings to fly. These two wings are: a focused one-pointed mind, and constant awareness of the spiritual goal of life. The mind has to be trained to go inward, to focus within. Until you have freed your mind from its habit of continually moving outward and have brought it under control, you will not progress in meditation. Spiritual practice is a definite art and science; the mind has to become sufficiently calm with focused concentration for spiritual experiences to follow.

The first step in focusing the mind for meditation is to give the mind a steady focal point. In Yoga Meditation it is usually the breath or a *mantra* (sacred sound) that is the focus for resting the mind's full attention to calm its distracting activities.

Once you have mastered sitting steadily in *āsana* (a comfortable and steady posture), and have regulated your breath, the mind or the attention flows in one direction, there is tremendous energy and your attention is not easily distracted and diverted.

Steps toward concentration for meditation

1) Relax the mind and body. The less tension there is in the mind and body, the easier it is for the mind to focus its attention. Relaxing the body in the correct posture is necessary for concentration because it allows the energies in the spine to flow upward to the higher brain centres without obstruction. Relaxation – the gate to openness and receptivity – helps to counteract the contractive force of the self-limited ego-sense.

2) Steady the mind and body. A steady pose gives concentration of mind. The practice of *Yoga āsanas* will enable you to regain steadiness of the body and mind, so that without distraction, the attention may be focused upon the object of concentration.

3) Calm the breathing. If you pay attention to your breathing, you will come to know the degree of distractedness of the mind. The less distracted it is, the calmer the breath. The practice of *prāṇāyāma* (Yoga breathing that regulates and harmonises the energy or subtle life force within the body) brings calmness and equilibrium to the mind, enabling it to concentrate without distraction. A very good breathing practice for this is alternate nostril breathing (*nāḍī śodhana prāṇāyāma*), also called *Anuloma Viloma* (see page 189).

4) Cultivate interest and attention. Concentration also requires interest and attention. We have to create interest to induce attention, because the mind finds it difficult to focus on an uninteresting object but easy to focus on an attractive one.

5) Focus on one idea alone. Train your mind to concentrate on God or the blissful Self within through the daily practice of deep meditation. Then as the mind experiences immense joy from the practice of one-pointed concentration, it will not be distracted by external objects. The more your mind is fixed on God or the Self within, the more inner strength and energy you will acquire.

6) Discipline your mind with daily *sādhanā* (spiritual practice). Concentration increases by reducing your activities; watching the mind and through enquiry into the nature of the Self; observing silence for one or two hours daily; remaining in seclusion for one or two hours daily; practising *prāṇāyāma*; cultivating mental non-attachment; self-restraint; and increasing the time sitting in meditation.

Fixing your mind on the Divine Self

The wise person should at all times attentively meditate upon the inner Self, which, though unseen, is yet the only reality, and, though manifest as the external universe, is yet of the nature of subjective consciousness.
Sri Sankaracharya

When all your mental energies are centred and concentrated on one single thought or idea, the senses become still, and the mind becomes calm and steady. The dissipated rays of the mind are collected and focused only on that one thought or idea. This is one-pointedness (*ekāgratā*) of mind. When the mind is confined and fixed steadily on a certain idea or object for a prolonged period that state is called *dhāraṇā* (concentration). As this state deepens, the practitioner gradually loses awareness of his or her surroundings. As the concentration is continued it leads to the state of meditation (*dhyāna*), in which the meditator forgets even his/her physical form. Concentration is the master key that opens the door to meditation, and ultimately to the superconscious state in which the meditator experiences divine bliss.

The Sanskrit word for bliss or joy is *Ānanda*, which is another name for the Self, for God – the one and only Reality of our being. The more we concentrate on our inner Self the more we are connected with *Ānanda*, our own natural joyful state of being. Those who experience in deep meditation their identity with God or Self know the fullness of that joy. Another Sanskrit word for the true nature of the God-Self within is *Sat-Cit-Ānanda*, which means Ever-existing, Ever-Conscious, Ever-new Bliss (Joy).

Hong Sau technique of concentration

An excellent technique for deepening the concentration and calming the mind in preparation for deep meditation is a technique in which you focus on the inhalation and exhalation with the two seed-syllable (*bīja*) mantra ***Hong Sau*** (pronounced as 'Hong-saw'). This *mantra* works on a pure vibrational level by stilling the mental energy in the form of restless thoughts and purifying the ego. *Hong Sau* is the inner sound of the inhaling and exhaling breath. It also calms and interiorises the *prāṇa* in the body.

The mind can never be focused without a mental object. Therefore you must give your mind an object that is readily available in every present moment. Your breath is the closest object. Every moment the breath is flowing in and flowing out through your nostrils. The concentration technique of *Hong Sau*, practised by deeply concentrating intently on the breath with total attention, trains the mind to stay focused like a 'one-pointed' laser beam. By training your mind to maintain a concentrated focus on a single point on the breath, while following it with the *mantra*, the other techniques and meditations that you practise will become increasingly deeper.

Hong Sau means 'I am He', 'I, the manifested Self, am He, the Unmanifested Spirit (the Absolute)'. By consciously repeating mentally the seed-syllable mantra **Hong Sau**, in conjunction with the concentration on the breath, we affirm that the ego-self is one with the Infinite Spirit. **Hong** as the inhaling breath represents the contraction of consciousness into finitude. **Sau** as the exhaling breath represents the expansion of consciousness and the reabsorption of differentiation and separation into pure unity.

Hong Sau is the natural sound of the breath – **Hong** with the inhalation, **Sau** with the exhalation. Throughout the 24 hours of the day the breath flows in and out 21,600 times in a continuous mantra of **Hong Sau**. Unknowingly, we are all repeating this mantra in a process of automatic and continuous recitation. In Yoga, continuous recitation of a mantra is called *ajapā-japa*. The *japa* becomes *ajapā* when the mantra gets repeated in the mind on its own. The difference between *ajapā-japa* and *japa* is that *ajapā-japa* goes on subconsciously all the time, while *japa* is done consciously.

The great *Kriya Yogi*, Paramhansa Yogananda (1893–1952) as a young boy named Mukunda, would sit in meditation and practise **Hong Sau** meditation technique for seven hours at a time, until he became breathless. He called **Hong Sau**, "the Baby *Kriya*." The actual *Kriya* meditation technique, that has been passed down through a succession of enlightened *Kriya* Masters from Mahavatar Babaji to Paramhansa Yogananda, the Kundalini life force flows in the spine and rises up through the *chakras* to the pituitary gland at the *ājñā* (the sixth chakra), and then it is offered to the Divine at the crown centre (*sahasrāra*) above the head.

> *The purpose of the Hong Sau technique is to help you to free your attention from outwardness, and to withdraw it from the senses, for breath is the cord that keeps the soul tied to the body... By dispassionately watching the breath coming in and going out, one's breathing naturally slows, calming at last the peace-disturbing activity of the heart, lungs, and diaphragm.*
> Paramhansa Yogananda

To prepare for this practice of Hong-Sau, follow this procedure:

1. Tensing and relaxing

Sit in a comfortable and steady meditation posture with the head, neck and spine aligned. Relax the mind and body by inhaling deeply and holding the breath. Then while retaining your breath, tense all the muscles in your body. Hold both the breath and the tension in the muscles for a few seconds, then simultaneously release the breath and the tension and relax. Repeat the process of tensing and relaxing three times, then finish by completely relaxing, and *feel* the relaxation and the flow of energy into the body.

2. Controlled breathing

Now continue to remain relaxed as you practise a minimum of

nine rounds of *loma prāṇāyāma*. This is a three-part equal breath ratio, breathing through both nostrils. Inhale for a count of 12, hold the breath for a count of 12, exhale for 12 (12:12:12). If this is not within your lung capacity, keeping the same ratio, halve it to 6:6:6. The number of rounds can be gradually increased over a period of time to 27 rounds.

3. Sit calmly for meditation

Remain sitting still and concentrate your relaxed attention at the point between the eyebrows (spiritual eye). Let go of all thoughts and be totally centred in the present here and now moment. Place your hands palms upward on the knees in *chin mudrā* (gesture of consciousness). Close your eyes and relax, with your awareness on the natural breath. Keep the body still and bring your attention and awareness to frontal part of the brain at the point between the eyebrows (the spiritual eye, the seat of spiritual consciousness). If your mind wanders, gently bring it back to the practice of watching the breath with awareness. Watching the breath is a present-moment experience. Interiorise your mind by deepening your attentive awareness and concentration.

Hong Sau – Technique of concentration

Now with your body and mind still, uniting your mind with the present moment, begin the practice *Hong Sau*. With closed eyes and without straining, gently lift your gaze upward to the point between the eyebrows, and with steady concentration and calmness look into the spiritual eye. Feel the natural breath flow in and out of the nostrils. Feel the tactile sensation of the breath, and try to feel where the flow of breath is strongest in the nostrils. The sensation of breath is subtle, and yet it is quite distinct when you learn to tune into it. Once you have found the point where the breath is the strongest in the nostrils (this is usually just inside the tip of the nose), then concentrate on the breath at that point. It is from this point that you will follow the whole passage of breath. Use this single point sensation inside the nose to keep your attention fixed. Observe each breath with attention and precision in present-moment awareness, taking it one split second on top of another. In this way, continuous and unbroken awareness will eventually result. Then begin to feel the sensation of the air that passes in and out of your nostrils higher up in the nasal passages by the point between the eyebrows, at the seat of concentration. As your concentration deepens your breathing will slow down, and you will be able to focus on it more clearly, with fewer and fewer interruptions. As you concentrate on your breath, make no attempt to control the breath. This is not a Yoga breathing exercise. Just let go and allow the natural process of breathing to go along at its own rhythm.

Inhale deeply, then slowly exhale. As the next inhalation naturally arises and flows into the nostrils, feel the breath where it enters the nostrils, and at the same time mentally repeat the *bīja* (seed-syllable) *mantra* **Hong** (rhymes with 'song'). Imagine that the breath itself is making this sound. And as the breath flows out naturally of its own accord, at the same time mentally repeat the *mantra* **Sau** (rhymes with 'saw'). Make no attempt to control the breath, just allow its flow to be completely natural. The process of ***Hong Sau*** is not a breathing technique; it is simply being consciously aware with the concentration on the **Hong Sau** *mantra* as the breath flows. Feel that the breath itself is silently making the sounds of **Hong Sau**. Continue gazing into the spiritual eye, the seat of spiritual consciousness, and as the breath naturally flows in simultaneously mentally repeat the *mantra* **Hong**. As the breath flows out, simultaneously mentally repeat the *mantra* **Sau**. By concentration on the breath, the breath gradually diminishes. This gradual subtle refinement leads naturally to an interiorised meditative state. When the mind is united with the breath flowing all the time, you will be able to focus the mind on the present moment.

As you practise **Hong Sau**, you may become aware that the

pauses or spaces between each breath are increasing. Follow your awareness: Now the breath is flowing in… Now the breath is still… Now the breath is flowing out… Now the breath is flowing in again… Now the breath is still… Be aware of this stillness between each breath. The stillness of the breath occurs at the point where the breath is retained, which occurs naturally at the point where the breath is held. As these pauses or intervals of breath suspension between the breaths grow longer, enjoy the meditative bliss and expansion into the freedom of infinite spaciousness while inwardly gazing into your spiritual eye. By silently observing the breathless state, you let go of the identification with your body, and realise that you are something other than the mind-body-senses. You realise that your body is sustained by something other than the breath. In the stillness in between breaths of the breathless state, you perceive the present moment of the Reality within you. This is the space of the innermost Self. Enjoy that experience of expansion into the freedom of infinite spaciousness while inwardly gazing into your spiritual eye. Then, when the breath naturally returns, continue with the practice of ***Hong-Sau***.

During and after practising ***Hong-Sau***, remain in the inner calmness for as long as possible. Remember and *feel* that inner calmness from your meditation, and remain calmly centred within your Self, allowing the calmness to permeate your everyday consciousness as you go about your daily activities.

The Breathless State

By silently observing the breathless state, you let go of the identification with your body, and realise that you are something other than mind-body-senses. You realise that your body is sustained by something other than the gross breath. In the perfect stillness in between the breaths of the breathless state, you perceive the reality of pure consciousness within you.

This breathless state, in which there are long pauses between the breaths, happens naturally. There is no need to be anxious or alarmed, for the breath returns automatically when the body needs to breathe again. Just remain calm and aware in the meditative stillness and inner freedom from body-consciousness, and allow the breath to effortlessly flow, stop and start naturally without any control by you.

Practising Hong Sau in Daily Life

Apart from sitting meditation, *Hong Sau* can be used effectively in daily living situations. Here are some different ways of using the *Hong Sau* technique:

At times other than meditation time

Practise *Hong Sau* during free or spare or at times other than meditation time – when you are not having to study, work, or do anything that requires your concentration such as travelling on public transport (train, bus, aircraft, or as a passenger in a car), and when you are sitting, waiting for your appointment (doctor, dentist) or an interview. As you sit resting, you can either keep your eyes closed (focused at the midpoint between the eyebrows) or open (focus your gaze on one point). Observe your breath mentally chanting *Hong* with the inhalation and *Sau* with the exhalation. This practice will help you to keep your mind calm and focused and free from mental restlessness.

When you are nervous, restless or agitated

Sometimes you may find yourself in a nervous, restless or agitated state. To calm the mind of these states sit quietly if possible and observe your breath, mentally repeat *Hong* as you inhale and *Sau* as you exhale. Even if you are outside walking, you can still calm your mind by observing your breath and mentally repeating *Hong Sau*.

When you are experiencing pain or suffering

If you are experiencing pain or suffering (physical, mental or emotional), observe your breath and mentally repeat *Hong* as you inhale and *Sau* as you exhale at the centre of the pain. This will help you to not identify yourself with the pain. It will help to reduce and may even dissolve the pain.

To resolve or solve a problem and to raise your consciousness

Hong Sau can also be practised to resolve or solve a problem, and to raise your consciousness. As you observe your breath, focus your attention at the medulla oblongata at the back of the brain (the centre of ego-consciousness), and as you inhale mentally repeat *Hong* and feel the energy gathering at the medulla. As you exhale, mentally repeat *Sau*, and offer the energy up to your spiritual eye (at the midpoint between the eyebrows).

Meditation begins with concentration

Meditation begins with concentration, for to enter the state of super-conscious meditation the mind must become calm, steady and one-pointed. Concentration is the key that opens the door to meditation, which requires repeated efforts of undaunted enthusiasm over a long period of time to attain success.

There is a difference between concentration and meditation. In concentration (*dhāraṇā*), the attention is focused on a small limited area (the object of concentration). If at that time only one thought or idea functions in the mind, that is meditation (*dhyāna*). In meditation there is not even a suggestion of distraction. If there is awareness of distraction, you are only concentrating, not meditating.

The difference between concentration and meditation is that in concentration there is a peripheral awareness and distraction, whereas in meditation the attention is not disturbed, there are no distractions at all. In meditation the mind becomes one with its object; it is only conscious of itself and the object.

Just as a flame sheltered from the wind burns bright and steady,

so shines the disciplined mind of a yogi practising concentration on the Self.
Bhāgavad Gīta 6:19

Meditation is a practical, scientific and systematic technique for realising the truth of the essential nature of who you are – the inner experience of the blissful Self. Meditation is a process of inner purification: it purifies the heart and cleanses the doors of perception to reveal what is already self-existent. Meditation is an inner journey from the distracted state of mind to a state of inner stillness; a journey to discovering, realising and establishing yourself in your own essential spiritual nature – the divine Self.

Meditation is the highest form of worship

Through meditation you learn how to disconnect your energy from the senses and consciously go into the Infinite. You experience an expansion of consciousness from the boundaries of the body to the boundaries of eternity.
Paramhansa Yogananda, *How to Awaken Your True Potential: The Wisdom of Yogananda, Volume 7*, Crystal Clarity Publishers, Nevada City, California, 2016

The divine inner Self is the true sacred shrine at which we worship when we meditate. You do not have to go on a devotional pilgrimage to the Himalayas or any other holy place to experience the grace and blessings of the Divine. The Divine is *within* you; your heart is your internal, portable sacred shrine that you carry with you every moment of your life. It is close to you as your very breath; wherever you are God *is*. You are always the Truth (Consciousness), and the Truth is changeless, self-luminous, one and indivisible. You have only to remove the obstacles – the activity of the ego-mind and the sense of separateness – that stop you from realising the Truth. When all obstacles are removed, the changeless, self-luminous 'I' (your real nature) remains over in all its glory. It is this 'I' or pure Awareness that illuminates all objects. When the objects of mind-ego are removed, what can I be but light itself? Where there is light, there can be no darkness.

Inner communion with God within

Inner communion with your true Self, the God or Divine within you, in the direct experience of meditation is the highest form of worship. There is also a distinction between prayer and meditation. In prayer there is a duality when it is offered to a divine personality or deity perceived as being separate from us. Whereas in meditation, it may begin with concentration on a sacred sound, symbol or image, but it always ends in absorption, unity in oneness with the Divine. In prayer we commune with the Divine by talking to God, but in meditation we *listen* to the pure Divine sound *Aum*, that represents God within us, and achieve blissful union with it. *Aum* takes you nearer to the Ultimate Truth. The more you listen to the repetition of *Aum*, the more you will become firmly established in the ultimate Reality. (See page 179 for '*Aum* Technique'.)

There are numerous names, words and symbols used to symbolise God. But there is no other word that can convey the significance and *direct* experience of the Ultimate Reality so profoundly and accurately as the word-sound symbol, *Aum* (*Oṁ*). Even the word God in comparison to *Aum* is insufficient and limited in its function and significance.

All the sacred scriptures born out of India, from the *Vedas* to the *Upaniṣads*, and from *Yoga* and *Vedanta*, maintain that the eternal Word *Aum* (the *Praṇava*) signifies the Supreme Reality. *Aum* is that which expresses the inexpressible. It is the true and highest symbol of *Brahman* both as the Absolute (God), and as the personal God (*Īśvara*), that has been chanted, contemplated and meditated upon by rishis, sages, and yogis down through the ages.

Aum transcends all the conceptions of symbols and anything that is signified by the symbols. *Aum* is a unique symbol; there is no other symbol that represents all the different aspects of the Ultimate Reality in one sound. It is all-inclusive; it includes all sounds, and all thoughts and concepts of God. The subtlest of all vibrations is *Aum*, the sound-form of the Ultimate Reality or God, that is omnipresent, omniscient, and omnipotent, and has infinite energy and power.

Aum Meditation Technique

> *Patañjali speaks of God (in the Yoga sūtras) as the actual Cosmic Sound of Aum heard in meditation. Aum is the Creative Word, the sound of the Vibratory Motor. Even the yogi-beginner soon inwardly hears the wondrous sound of AUM. Receiving this blissful spiritual encouragement, the devotee becomes assured that he is in actual touch with divine realms.*
> Paramhansa Yogananda, *Autobiography of a Yogi*, 1994 reprint of the original 1946 Edition, Crystal Clarity Publishers, Nevada City, CA

> *Kriya prāṇāyāma and contemplation of Oṁ are the keys to effective meditation practice. Practice of these methods make possible the fulfilment of one's highest aspirations.*
> Lahiri Mahasaya (1828–1895)

The *Aum* Technique will help you to inwardly attune with the Vibratory Sound of Cosmic Consciousness. *Aum* is the connecting link between human consciousness and Divine Cosmic Consciousness.

The *Aum* Technique can be practised at any time after the preliminary technique – *Hong Sau* – or it can be practised alone. During the peaceful energy of the night is particularly good for doing the *Aum* Technique.

This meditation of listening to the inner Vibratory Sound of *Aum* (*Oṁ*) is best practised when your mind is calm and focused in stillness after practising the *Hong Sau* technique (see page 171). Practise *Hong Sau* for at least three months, to help you deepen your concentration and calm the restlessness of the mind, before you start to practise this *Aum* inner sound meditation. Then you will be able to go deep in your meditation to feel a deep sense of inner calm, and attunement in oneness with the Divine Self.

Preparation

Before you practise the *Aum* meditation technique begin with a few rounds of *anuloma-viloma prāṇāyāma* (see page 189). Then focus and calm your mind by practising the *Hong Sau* technique for 10–15 minutes, or until you are calmly centred within in inner stillness.

Aum Technique

Sit in a meditation posture that is comfortable and steady, with your head, neck and spine aligned straight. Place your upper arms on a suitable armrest (like the T-shaped armrest in the picture, or sit with your knees together, pulled up against your chest, and rest your elbows on your knees). When using the T-shaped armrest, make sure your upper arms are resting parallel to the floor with your elbows in line with your shoulders. Make sure your arms and shoulders are at a comfortable height; there should be no strain on your hands, arms, back or neck.

Raise your hands up to your head and position your fingers in the *Aum Mudrā*: first close your ears by gently pressing the earflaps (*tragi*) inward with your thumbs. Rest your little fingers gently and lightly on the outer corners of each closed eyelid to stabilise the eyeballs. Rest your other fingers upward on your forehead, pointing inward toward the eyebrow centre (midpoint between the eyebrows), to direct energy toward the spiritual eye.

Breathe normally while holding the position of the *Aum Mudrā*, and with your eyes closed, gaze with deep attentive awareness into your spiritual eye. Then, in a natural rhythm, mentally chant *Aum, Aum, Aum, Aum*… continuously at the spiritual eye, so that the *mantra* vibrates and resonates in that centre. The correct pronunciation of *Aum (Oṁ)* is like the 'ong' in 'song' but drawn out and with the 'o' pronounced like its alphabet name. *Oṁ* is a pure vowel sound and the 'm' is silent, because the 'o' sound is prolonged.

As you gaze inwardly, into the spiritual eye mentally chanting *Aum*, with intuitive awareness, simultaneously listen in your right ear for the subtle sound frequencies of your *chakras*. If you hear one distinct sound, focus your awareness totally on that one sound. As sensitivity develops, another fainter sound will be heard behind it. Leave the first sound and transfer your awareness to the fainter sound. Again, a third sound will begin to emerge behind the second sound. With awareness continue discarding the grosser sounds for the more subtle sounds. Your aim is to reach the source of all sound – the Primordial Vibratory Sound, *Aum*.

> *In the beginning stage of the practice, one hears different types of strong or gross inner sounds. When the practice increases one hears subtle and subtler sounds.*
> Nādabindūpaniṣad 33

Try to hear the *Aum* sound first in your right ear, then going deeper, hear it in both your ears, until you hear it in the centre of your brain. Then, feel it gradually descending down to permeate every cell in your whole body, and then expanding outward. As your listening to *Aum* deepens, your consciousness expands, and you begin to feel omnipresent, beyond the ego, mind, body and senses. Your consciousness dissolves into that omnipresent *Aum* sound current of the power of Consciousness, and you feel complete oneness with *Aum*, experiencing bliss in the Supreme Consciousness.

After listening to the inner sound vibration of *Aum*, remain sitting for some time, calmly and joyfully in the stillness of your meditation, and experience pure awareness of Being or a perception of oneness with the Divine.

The Chakra Sounds as heard in Meditation

As a beginner, when you first practise the ***Aum* Inner Sound Meditation** you may only hear the inner sounds of the physical body: heartbeat, blood circulation and breathing. You may also hear a very high-pitched electrical sound from the electrical field of energy of the astral body. If you hear any of these distinct sounds, then concentrate on them until they recede into the background, then transfer your awareness to the next fainter sound that you hear, and then to the more subtle astral sounds. If your mind is deeply interiorised and calm while listening to these inner sounds, you will eventually be able to tune into and hear the subtle sounds of the *chakras*. Listening to the inner *chakra* sounds will lead you to hear the Primordial Sound vibration, *Aum*.

Muladhara Chakra – The humming or drone of bees, a low vibratory sound. When heard less perfectly it may sound like a motor or a drum.

Svādhiṣṭhāna Chakra – Like a flute. When heard less perfectly it may sound like crickets (sound made by the wings beating of the cricket insect), or running water.

Manipura Chakra – Stringed instrument sound like a sitar or a harp.
Anāhata Chakra – Like the flowing peal of deep bells or a gong. Less perfectly it sounds like tinkling bells.
Viśuddha Chakra – Thunder or the roar of an ocean. When heard less perfectly it may sound like the wind or a waterfall.
Ājñā Chakra (spiritual eye/medulla) – A symphony of sounds; *Aum*.

Brahman is beyond the silence, the state is of the Supreme Self (Paramātmā). While there is sound there is the mind, at the end of sounds the mind does not exist.
Nādabindūpaniṣad 48

When the mind concentrates on the subtle inner sounds, it recognises the different types of sounds, but still the mind has not been transcended. It is only when the mind completely merges with the subtle sounds that both the subtle sounds and the mind cease to exist. The ultimate goal is for the Self (*Ātmān*) to merge in the *Brahman* (God) the universal Consciousness, 'That' which is beyond all sounds, and which is to be known and realised.

All that we experience and perceive in this world is dependent upon there being both a subject and an object, or a seer and a seen. Nothing can be experienced or perceived without the subject, the seer. And vice-versa, if there is no object, but only a subject or seer to perceive it, nothing is experienced. If a tree falls in the stillness of a forest, and no one hears it fall, was there really a sound?

Superconscious Yoga Meditation

The scientific interior process of Superconscious Yoga Meditation is the key to opening the *chakras* (seven centres of consciousness and energy in the subtle spine). The meditator regulating his or her mind and heart through self-discipline disconnects the mind from the outward senses and their objects of distraction. Then by bringing the mind to the present moment and making the mind single-pointed by chanting the mantra *Aum*, first aloud and then mentally, the attention is shifted from the chanting to the silence underlying it. The attention is then interiorised within, and by deeply concentrating at the point between the eyebrows at the spiritual eye, the consciousness and life force are withdrawn from the bodily consciousness of the lower *chakras*, and directed upwards through the astral spine (*suṣumnā*) to the thousand-rayed lotus in the *sahasrāra chakra*, at the crown of the head. There the individual self or soul is freed and united in blissful superconsciousness or absorption (*samādhi*).

A Guided Deep Meditation

1. Sit in a meditation posture that is steady and comfortable, with your head, neck and spine upright and aligned. To relax your body, first inhale deeply through the nose and, while holding your breath, tense all the muscles in your body. Then, with a deep double exhalation (ha-haaa) through your mouth relax your whole body. Repeat this exercise three times.

   Then remain still, relax and feel the energy flow into your body. Take a few silent moments to invoke the presence of the Divine by praying in the language of your heart, before you start your meditation. For example: *"Divine Mother, Heavenly Father, Infinite Spirit... May Your Divine Grace enliven my body, mind and spirit, and inspire, bless and guide my meditation, to fill me with inner clarity, love, peace and joy."*
2. Now, with your eyes closed, gently move your spine left and right by swaying your body, changing the centre of your consciousness from the physical body and senses to your inner astral spine. With awareness, feel the inner subtle astral spine (*suṣumnā*) and stop swaying your body. Then feel your consciousness and energy travel up and down

through your spine several times, with the inhalation and exhalation, from the coccygeal plexus at the base of your spine to the point between your eyebrows.

3. Imagine and feel your spine to be like a spacious hollow tube that runs from the base of your spine at the coccyx to the medulla oblongata at the top of your spine, and then arcs forward to connect with the point between your eyebrows.
4. Continue to keep your eyes closed, and with a steady inner gaze, concentrate at the midpoint between your eyebrows, the centre of spiritual consciousness. Then become aware of your breath's natural rhythm; do not try to control it in any way, just be aware of each breath as it flows in and out. Notice where your inhalation and exhalation arise and dissolve. Be still, and remain calmly centred within as you continue to gaze into your spiritual eye while being aware of your natural breath.
5. Focus your attention on your own awareness, as if you are being attentive to attention on your awareness, as if you are being attentive to attention itself. Be that awareness in the present-now-moment, and become aware of that part of you that is witnessing your experience – your inner Self. The Self knows itself; it is a witness to its own existence.
6. Now breathe in using the *ujjayi prāṇāyāma* (see page 188), with the air directed in the back of your throat, so that it is slightly expanded to create a suction effect. And as you inhale, be aware of the cool sensation that you feel in your throat. Transfer that cool sensation to your inner subtle spine as you inhale up the spine.
7. Inhaling deeply in *ujjayi prāṇāyāma* (to a count of 10–15) making a soft sibilant breathing sound (without using your vocal cords) deep in your expanded throat (that only you can hear), pull a cool current of *prāṇic* energy from the base of your spine up to your medulla oblongata (the negative pole of the spiritual eye) and across into the midpoint

between your eyebrows (the positive pole of the spiritual eye). The inhalation should be smooth and continuous without any interruptions in it.

8. After drawing the inhaling breath up your spine to the eyebrow centre, pause and hold your breath with a mental count of three *Aums*.
9. Now exhale slowly and deeply in *ujjayi* breath (to a count of 10–15). As you do this let your attentive awareness feel the warm sensation of the breath as it moves down through the spine from your eyebrow centre to the coccygeal plexus at the base of your spine.
10. Then without a pause begin to inhale up your spine – repeat the whole process as before. Practise 12 cycles of this deep breathing up and down your spine. Magnetise your spine with energy by concentrating on drawing energy into it with each breath, particularly with the inhaling breath.
11. Then when you feel your spine is sufficiently magnetised, and vibrating and pulsating with *prāṇic* energy or life force, to become aware of the inner currents of life force in the spine that correspond to the physical breath, practise a more subtle breathing in your astral spine (*suṣumnā*) by adding the mantra *Hong-Sau*. But, this time drop the *ujjayi prāṇāyāma*, breathe normally, and allow your breath to naturally follow its own course. There must be no control of your breath. Just observe your consciousness-awareness moving up and down, deep in your spine, between the base of the spine, the medulla oblongata, and the eyebrow centre. Follow the movement of your breath and listen to the inner sound it makes. As you breathe in, mentally repeat *Hong* as the energy and awareness moves up the spine, and as you breathe out mentally repeat *Sau* as it moves down. Think of your astral spine as a tunnel of light, and concentrate on feeling the energy in your astral spine rising and falling with the inhalation and exhalation (the astral breath).

12. With attentive focus listen to the seed syllables of the mantra: *Hong* with the inhalation and upward energy in your spine, and *Sau*, with the exhalation and downward energy, as you mentally repeat them. Merge your attention with the flow of breath, and identify yourself more and more with the vibration and energy of the *mantra*. To do this, feel the Divine Consciousness in *Hong Sau*, and sense or visualise the *Hong Sau* mantra as light or energy, and see and feel yourself immersed in it, until you feel you have become one with it and are blessed by it. Mentally affirm: "I am Spirit, I am Pure I-Awareness, the ever-Existing, ever-Conscious, ever-Blissful Self." With your mind calm and peaceful, remain in the stillness of meditation with a deep feeling of devotional self-offering, and the awareness of Divine Presence, for as long as you naturally can, feeling the experience of expansion of consciousness and oneness in the Divine.

Closing your meditation

Now return to normal breathing, and to make the transition from inner space to a grounded outer focus, gradually become aware of the sensation of your physical body. Then fold your hands together in the prayer *mudrā* (*Anjali Mudrā*) and offer gratitude to the Source of the Divine within you, for Its grace, blessings, energy and power, that allows you to inwardly unfold your consciousness. Then chant:

Oṁ Śhānti (Peace) three times, sending peace and love to all beings in the universe. Let every breath that flows from you create a strong current of universal and divine service for all beings. Slowly open your eyes, then remain quietly seated for some time to enjoy the calm and peace from your meditation. Allow this inner calmness to permeate into your everyday consciousness as you go about your work, study and duties.

Part Five

Yoga Practices for Meditation

Prāṇāyāma

Prāṇāyāma is the fourth limb of *Aṣṭāṅga Yoga* (Eight Limbs of Raja Yoga), as outlined in the ancient text of Patañjali's *Yoga Sūtras*.

The Sanskrit word *prāṇāyāma* is formed by two words: *prāṇa* means energy or subtle life force that permeates and sustains all life; *ayāma* has two meanings: to regulate, and to extend, lengthen or expand. *Prāṇāyāma* means regulating and harmonising the energy or subtle life force within the body. *Prāṇa* is not breath in the gross form, and *prāṇāyāma* is not just regulating or controlling the breath, but direct perception of the life principle.

Prāṇa is the universal force of nature and the energy that pervades the entire physical system that acts as a medium between the body and the mind. *Prāṇa* is more subtle than the physical body but grosser than the mind.

By the process of *prāṇāyāma*, individual energy and consciousness are expanded into universal energy and consciousness.

Patañjali says we should have a steady posture (*āsana*) before attempting *prāṇāyāma*, because when you practise, the *prāṇa* vibrates more powerfully. The posture has to be steady and comfortable, and the mind concentrated on the Infinite. When this is accomplished, the body and mind become stable. Then the breath can be easily suspended for extended periods of time.

Ujjayi prāṇāyāma (victorious breath)

1. Sit in a comfortable and stable meditation posture with the head, neck and spine aligned. Relax the mind and body by taking a few deep breaths. Inhale deeply and tense the whole body, then exhale and let go of all tension from the body and completely relax. Place your hands palms down on the knees in *jñana mudrā* (gesture of knowledge). Close your eyes and relax, with your awareness on the natural breath.

2. Now **inhale** slowly with a smooth, deep and continuous *ujjayi* breath. (Close the mouth and inhale through the nasal passages with the glottis partially closed. The glottis is the opening between the vocal chords, at the upper part of the windpipe. This causes the air to rush past the partly closed glottis, producing a soft sound within the throat. The passage of the incoming air is felt on the roof of the palate and makes an 'aaah' sound or the aspirate sound of 'ha'.) During the inhalation keep the abdominal muscles slightly contracted. Completely expand the lungs with air by raising and expanding the ribs until the chest is expanded forward like a victorious warrior.
3. Now **exhale** slowly with a smooth, deep and continuous *ujjayi* breath through both nostrils. The outgoing breath makes a sibilant 'sa', 'so', or 'sau' sound. During exhalation the abdominal muscles will naturally be more contracted. The duration of the exhalation is always longer than the inhalation, usually in the proportionate ratio of 1:2. This means that if you inhale for five seconds, exhalation should be ten seconds.
4. Practise 5–20 rounds of *Ujjayi prāṇāyāma*, starting with five and increasing by two rounds each week until you reach 20.

Nāḍī śodhana* or *Anuloma Viloma prāṇāyāma

The breath is a vehicle for deepening concentration and bringing the mind to a state of calm and inner stillness. Alternate Nostril Breathing (*Nāḍī śodhana* or *Anuloma Viloma*) is an excellent primary revitalising Yoga breathing practice that relaxes the mind, deepens self-awareness in preparation for meditation, opens the flow of *prāṇic* energy in the *nāḍīs* (subtle energy channels) and purifies the *nāḍīs* of impurities, balances the left and right hemispheres of the brain, equalises the flow of energy in the *iḍā* and *piṅgala nāḍīs* – the left, lunar and right solar subtle energy channels located on either side of the central channel (*suṣumnā nāḍī*) that twines upward through the spine, intersecting at each *chakra*. *Iḍā* ends in the left nostril; *piṅgala* terminates in the right.

Śodhana (pronounced as *shodana*) in Sanskrit means 'to purify'. This is the alternate nostril breathing *prāṇāyāma* that maintains equilibrium in the catabolic and anabolic processes in the body. It purifies the blood and the brain cells. It brings consistency and regularity to our patterns of breathing, and it has a calming effect on the nervous system.

A smooth and unobstructed flow of *prāṇa* is needed for concentration and meditation. For the yogi it is usual to make the breath flow equally in each nostril. When the flow of air is equal in each nostril, then the flow in the *iḍā* and *piṅgala nāḍīs* are also equalised – they become balanced. Under these balanced conditions, *prāṇa* begins to flow in the central main *suṣumnā nāḍī*, influencing all the *chakras*, and the mind becomes centred and still for the purpose of entering into meditation – calm awareness of the inner Self.

Method

1. Sit in any comfortable meditation pose, with the head, neck and spine aligned straight. Close the eyes and relax the whole body. Keep the body still and bring your attention and awareness to the point between the eyebrows at the spiritual eye (*ājñā chakra*).

2. Place your left hand palm upwards relaxed on your left knee. Raise your right hand (in *Viṣṇu mudrā*, an energy seal that helps to contain *prāṇa* within the body) with the palm in front of your face, and fold down your middle and index fingers into the palm, keeping the thumb and ring and little fingers extended. Alternatively, you can place your hand in *nāsikāgra mudrā* (index and second finger positioned at the eyebrow centre. Use thumb to open and close right nostril and the third finger to open and close left nostril).
3. **Exhale and close the right nostril** with your thumb. **Inhale slowly, smoothly and deeply through the left nostril.** Pause.
4. **Close the left nostril** with the ring finger and slowly **exhale through the right nostril**. Pause.
5. **Inhale through the right nostril.** Pause.
6. Close the right nostril with your thumb and **exhale through the left nostril.**

This completes one round. Begin with 5 to 10 rounds and over a period of time gradually increase to 20 rounds. Practise twice daily – morning and evening on an empty or light stomach. When doing a complete Yoga practice session, practise alternate nostril breathing just after *āsanas* and prior to meditation.

Breathing Ratios for Beginners

It is advised to start with the 1:2:2 breath ratio for a few months before taking up the advanced ratio 1:4:2. For beginners this means that the breath retention is twice that of the inhalation, and the duration of exhalation is the same as that of the retention. For advanced students it means that the breath retention is four times that of the inhalation, and the duration of exhalation is twice that of the inhalation.

The minimum starting proportion for a beginner is 4:8:8. After having practised this ratio for one month, then increase the ratio to

5:10:10. Then increase gradually until you reach 8:16:16. On no account should you increase this proportion until you are able to practise it with comfort and ease. You must *never* force, strain or interrupt the overall rhythm of your breathing practice; to do so could cause strain and injury to the physical body. If your next breath is gasping or hurried, then you have certainly held the breath for too long. Always seek advice from an experienced and qualified teacher who practises *prāṇāyāma*.

Alternate nostril breathing with the mantra *Sohaṁ-haṁsa*

The Sanskrit mantra *haṁsa* means 'I am He' (the Self, Consciousness), when repeated constantly it seems to become *So'haṁ*, which means 'He (the Absolute) am I'. Either way it has the same meaning. Inhaling with *haṁ* represents the contraction of consciousness into finitude. Exhaling with *Sa* represents the expansion of consciousness and the resorption of differentiation into pure unity. If you take out the *'s'* and the *'ha'* from the mantra *so'haṁ*, you are left with *'oṁ'* (*Aum*), the Primordial Sound Vibration (*Praṇava*) that represents God, that which sustains everything: the supreme Self.

In this exercise, the alternate breathing quietens the mind and the mental repetition of the mantra affirms your real innermost nature as the Self or Consciousness. It brings the yogi to Self-realisation.

Method

1. Sit in any comfortable meditation pose, with the head, neck and spine aligned straight. Close the eyes and relax the whole body. Keep the body still and bring your attention and awareness to the point between the eyebrows at the spiritual eye (*ājñā chakra*).
2. Place your left hand palm upwards relaxed on your left knee. Raise your right hand (in *Viṣṇu mudrā*, an energy seal that helps to contain *prāṇa* within the body) with the palm

in front of your face, and fold down your middle and index fingers into the palm, keeping the thumb and ring and little fingers extended. Alternatively, you can place your hand in *nāsikāgra mudrā* (index and second finger positioned at the eyebrow centre. Use the thumb to open and close the right nostril and the third finger to open and close the left nostril).

3. Exhale and close the right nostril with your thumb. Inhale slowly, smoothly and deeply through the left nostril, while at the same time mentally repeating the mantra *"**So**."* Pause.
4. Close the left nostril with the ring finger and slowly exhale through the right nostril, while at the same time mentally repeating the mantra *"**Haṁ**."* Pause.
5. Inhale through the right nostril, while at the same time mentally repeating the mantra *"**Haṁ**."* Pause.
6. Close the right nostril with your thumb and exhale through the left nostril, while at the same time mentally repeating the mantra *"**Sa**."*

This completes one round. Begin with 5 to 10 rounds and over a period of time gradually increase to 20 rounds. Practise twice daily – morning and evening on an empty or light stomach.

After practising the *sohaṁ-haṁsa* mantra with the alternate nostril breathing, then sit calmly with your mind focused at the spiritual eye (midpoint between the eyebrows on the forehead) in quiet meditation. Abide in the stillness of your real inner nature, the changeless Self, that is *Sat-Cit-Ānanda*, that is beyond the body, senses and mind.

Epilogue

Come out of your closed chamber of limitation. Breathe in the fresh air of vital thoughts.

Exhale poisonous thoughts of discouragement, discontentment, or hopelessness. Never suggest to your mind human limitations of sickness, old age, or death, but constantly remind yourself,

"I am the Infinite, which has become the body."

Paramhansa Yogananda, *How to Awaken Your True Potential: The Wisdom of Yogananda, Volume 7*, Crystal Clarity Publishers, Nevada City, CA, 2015

The mind is the creator of your body, thoughts and your circumstances. When your mind is restless, emotions are unstable, and concentration is unfocused, perception of your true essential nature and higher realities are flawed or obscured, preventing you from knowing the truth of your essential timeless nature or perfect Being (*Sat-Cit-Ānanda* – ever-existent, ever-conscious, ever-new Bliss).

Until all false notions that confuse the mind, and change and limit awareness are discarded or replaced with understanding, errors in discernment will continue to occur. The greatest error is presuming that a mistaken sense of identity (the ego-self misidentified with body, mind, personality characteristics, perceptions, stored impressions, and likes and dislikes) is your real nature. When that *mistaken* idea is firmly held, you fall under the illusion that the body-mind, and material world and its objects is the only reality, and that physical death is the end of your existence. This places you in a condition of great limitation.

This mistaken identity is due to forgetfulness of your eternal spiritual nature. As Paramhansa Yogananda instructed, "You have forgotten that your kingdom is omnipresence. You are omnipresent. Your home is eternity. You have unlimited power; you must cultivate that power. Meditation is the way to resurrect your soul from the bondage of the body and all your trials."

The minutes are more important than the years. If you fill the minutes of your life with thoughts of God, you will find the years

> *of your life automatically saturated with the consciousness of God.*
> Paramhansa Yogananda, *How to Awaken Your True Potential: The Wisdom of Yogananda, Volume 7*, Crystal Clarity Publishers, Nevada City, CA, 2015

Every moment of your life provides opportunities for life-enhancing discoveries. You have the potential and power to transform your mind and to know and realise your God-Self nature now. It only needs your intention, willingness, sincere desire and determination to succeed. Life has to be lived, so live it in the highest way. The whole life is *Yoga*. You are not required to live a spiritual life separated from living in the world. Living a spiritual life is living wisely in the world – performing your duties and serving and relating to others with love, kindness, compassion and respect – with a spiritual consciousness.

Spiritual Guidelines

- With sincerity and respectful attitude make a steady and long-term commitment to your spiritual practice routine (Yoga and meditation) – practise regularly and consistently, so that you become firmly grounded in it. Remember, Yoga is both the practice and the goal. It is both the way to bring the mind to stillness and the state of enlightenment and freedom.
- Your mind is an instrument of consciousness through which you experience your existence in this world. Train and master your mind; be the master of your mind that it may serve you wisely and effectively.
- Develop your concentration. When concentration becomes prolonged and deepened, it becomes meditation.
- Discipline your body, mind and senses. Without self-discipline the body-mind becomes restless and an obstacle to realising the Self.

- To help still the mind practise the two principles given in Patañjali's *Yoga Sūtras*: *abhyāsa* (continuous, disciplined and persistent practice); and *vairāgya* (dispassion, freedom from desire, detachment). These two principles work together to quieten the mind and enable one to progress forward toward spiritual enlightenment. The goal of all spiritual practice is to change your identification from the body, mind and senses to the ever-present and changeless inner Self. The realisation of your own real nature is the ultimate goal of all spiritual quests.
- Overcome habits of thinking, wrong attitudes and behaviour that are not useful or which are harmful.
- Aspire to be spiritually aware – cultivate Self- and God-awareness. You can only truly know God as the Self; otherwise knowledge of God is indirect and not real.
- You are always the Truth, and the Truth is Self-luminous; you have only to remove the obstacles of separateness and its objects so that the ever-existent, changeless luminous Self remains ever shining, just as the sun shines in all its glory as soon as the clouds are removed.
- Know who you are and know your divine purpose in life. Know that you are a spiritual Being expressing life through the material instruments of the body, mind and senses. Daily affirm that you are not the body, mind or the senses, and that even when all these are changing in the course of the three states – waking, dream and sleep – you alone stand changeless as the background, knowing the apparent changes. You are a divine Being with great potential and extraordinary abilities. It is up to you to release the divine power within you.
- Live wisely and effectively while maintaining your Self-knowing and clarity of awareness.
- Adhere to regimens of positive thinking, healthy diet, right living and daily spiritual practice.

- When you pray the only thing you need to pray for and hold on to without ceasing is the truth of your Divine nature.
- Meditate deeply every day of your life – stay attuned to that higher Consciousness, that one Power and Presence that is always within you – and abide in our own true nature, the Self. To attain true freedom is to identify oneself with that light of consciousness – the real Self within, that pure awareness that is aware of itself alone. This means you must give up the attachment to body, mind and senses. After practising your meditation techniques it is important to sit and rest in the *stillness* and simply *Be*, with focused attention on the Infinite. Expand your consciousness.
- Cultivate love for the Divine – love means becoming one with the object of your love. When both are *one*, there is no one to give and no one to take; there is only supreme Love. *Ānanda* (joy, bliss) is manifest as love when related to an object. Wherever there is love there is wholeness. The nature of the Self is love. The love and happiness that you experience is the Self alone. Without love you cannot understand, and without understanding you cannot love.

Guide to Sanskrit Pronunciation

Too often, in Western books on *Yoga*, there is an oversimplification of translation of a Sanskrit word into English, where the original meaning tends to get diluted, mistranslated, or lost. In this book I have tried to keep as many Sanskrit words as possible in their original meaning.

Since the late 18th century, Sanskrit has been transliterated using the Latin alphabet. The system most commonly used today is the IAST (International Alphabet of Sanskrit Transliteration), which has been the academic standard since 1888/1912.

The following guide to pronunciation gives approximate equivalents in English to the Sanskrit sounds.

Diacritical marks used in this translation

ā ī ū ṛ ḷ ḥ ṁ ṅ ñ ṇ ṭ ḍ ś ṣ

Vowels

a ā i ī u ū r ṛ ṝ l ḹ e ai o au

These vowels are further divided into simple vowels (*a*, *ā*, and so on) and combined vowels (*e*, *ai*, *o*, *au*). The simple vowels are listed in pairs (*a-ā*, *i-ī*...). In each pair the first vowel is short and the second is exactly twice as long. In the English transliteration the long vowels are marked with a bar (-). The diphthongs are also pronounced twice as long as the short vowels. Thus in the words *nī – la* 'blue' or *go – pa* 'cowherd', the first syllable is held twice as long as the second.

Simple

a short *a* as in '**a**bout'
ā long *a* as in 'f**a**ther'
i short *i* as **e** in '**e**ngland'

ī long *i* as in **ee** in 'f**ee**t'

u short *u* as in **oo** in 'f**oo**t'

ū long *u* as in 'r**u**le'

ṛ as in 'w**ri**tten' (but held twice as long)

ḷ **le** as in 'turt**le**'

ḹ longer '**le**'

Diphthongs

e as in 'they'

ai as in '**ai**sle' '**i**ce' 'k**i**te'

o as in 'go'

au as in '**ow**l'

Aspiration

ḥ (*visarga*) a final 'h' sound that echoes the preceding vowel slightly; as in 'aha' for ***aḥ***; ***iḥ*** as ihi; ***uḥ*** as uhu.

Nasalised vowel

ṁ (*anusvara* – marked with a dot) a nasal sound pronounced like *mm*, but influenced according to whatever consonant follows, as in 'bingo'. The nasal is modified by the following consonant: *sāṁkhya* as saankhya.

Consonants

Consonants are generally pronounced as in English, but there are some differences. Sanskrit has many 'aspirated' consonants; these are pronounced with a slight *h* sound. For example, the consonant *ph* is pronounced as English *p* followed by an *h* as in ha*ph*azard. The *bh* is as in a*bh*or.

k as in 's**k**ip'

kh as in 'E**ck**hart'

g as in '**g**ame'

gh as in 'do**gh**ouse'

ṅ as in 'si**ng**'

c	as in 'ex**ch**ange'
ch	as in '**ch**urch'
j	as in '**j**am'
jh	a in 'he**dg**ehog'
ñ	as in 'ca**n**yon'
ṭ	as in '**tu**b', the tongue curls back and hits the upper palate
ṭh	as in 'ligh**t-h**eart', the tongue curls back and hits the upper palate
ḍ	as in '**dove**', the tongue curls back and hits the palate
ḍh	as in 'a**dh**ere', the tongue curls back and hits the palate
ṇ	as in 'ti**n**t', tip of tongue touches the back of the upper teeth
t	as in 'tub', tip of tongue touches the back of the upper teeth
th	as in '**th**ick', tip of tongue touches the back of the upper teeth
d	as in '**d**ove', tip of tongue touches the back of the upper teeth
dh	as in 're**d-h**ot', tip of tongue touches the back of the upper teeth
n	as in '**n**ame', tip of tongue touches the back of the upper teeth
p	as in '**pap**a'
ph	as in 'ha**ph**azard'
b	as in '**b**alloon'
bh	as in 'a**bh**or'
m	as in '**m**um'
y	as in '**y**ellow'
r	as in '**r**un'
l	as in '**l**ove'
v	as in '**v**ine'
ś	as in '**sh**ell'
ṣ	as in '**s**ilk'
h	as in '**h**ill'

Double consonants

In double consonants, both letters are pronounced distinctly separately.

śraddhā (faith) is pronounced *śrad-dhā*

icchā (desire) is pronounced *ic-chā*

jagannātha (Lord of the Universe) is pronounced *jagan-nātha*

jña

jña (to know) as in *jñana Yoga* (the path of wisdom or higher knowledge) is widely pronounced 'gya'. More accurate is 'gnya', and best is to combine a correct *ja* with a correct *ña*.

Sanskrit Glossary

A

Abhiniveśa – Clinging to life; fear of death.

Abhyāsa – Persistent repeated practice.

Ācāryopāsanaṁ – Service to the Guru.

Adāmbhitvam – Unpretentiousness.

Ādhibautika – Caused by other beings.

Ādhidaivika – Caused by natural elemental forces.

Ādhyātmika – Within oneself.

Ahaṁkāra – *Aham* literally means 'I', as undivided Consciousness, and *Akara* means a shape or form. In this sense, *Ahaṁkāra* means the formless unlimited Consciousness that appears as a form with limitations. Identifying faculty; ego; the sense of 'I' or personal identity.

Ahiṁsā – Non-harming; non-violence.

Ājñā chakra – The sixth centre of consciousness located at the eyebrow centre in the astral body.

Ajñāna – Ignorance.

Alabdha-bhumikatva – Non-achievement of a Yogic state.

Ālasya – Laziness.

Amānitvam – Humility.

Anāhata chakra – The fourth centre of consciousness located at the heart centre in the astral body.

Ānanda – Bliss, Joy.

Antaḥkaraṇa – *Antah* means internal; *karana* means instrument, the 'internal instrument' (*manas, buddhi*, *ahaṁkāra*, *citta*), located in the subtle body. That which works within; human psyche.

Antarāya – Obstacles and impediments.

Aratiḥ janasaṁsadi – Disinclination for worldly society.

Asaktiḥ – Non-attachment.

Asaṁprajñāta samādhi – Superconsciousness beyond (perfect) knowledge. The Self dwelling in its own true nature as the Self.

Ashta-prakritis – Earth, water, fire, air, ether, mind, intellect and ego.

Asmitā – *Asmi* means 'I am'. *Asmitā* is the sense of individuality, the principle of egoism; 'I-sense', 'I-am-ness'. *Asmitā* the effect of *buddhi* evolves out of ignorance (*avidyā* – the root cause of all other *kleśas*).

Asmitā kleśa – Affliction of ego.

A-sthira – Unsteady.

Ātmān – The Self.

Ātmavinigrahaḥ – Mastery over the mind.

Avidyā – Ignorance. A mental state or perception which misidentifies the nature of the Self with that of the body. The first of the five *kleśas* (afflictions – *avidyā*, *asmitā*, *rāga*, *dveṣa* and *abhiniveśa*) and the ground for all of them.

Avirati – Inability to withdraw the mind from sense cravings.

B

Bandha – Literally translates as 'lock'. *Bandhas* are inner actions that direct the subtle power of the breath or *prāṇa*, locking it into a particular part of the body.

Bhrānti-darśana – Delusion.

Brahmamuhurta – The auspicious time between the early hours of 4:00am and 6:00am, when the natural atmosphere is charged with *prāṇic* energy and the qualities of peacefulness and goodness (*sattva*).

Buddhi – From *budh*, 'to wake up', 'be aware of '. Intellect; intelligence; discriminating or determinative faculty that contains intuitive wisdom.

C

Chakra – Wheel, vortex of energy, energy centre within the body, of which there are seven main centres. The *chakras* are transformers for the *prāṇic* life-energy and consciousness flowing through them. They store energy and distribute it throughout the body.

Chanchala – Restless.

Citta – *Cit* means 'to perceive', 'be conscious'. The totality of the mind; field of consciousness that includes the three cognitive functions: *buddhi*, *ahaṁkāra* and *manas*; mind; *citta* stores impressions and experiences.

Citta vikṣepa – Distractors of the mind.

D

Darśanam – 'Keeping in sight'.

Deśa – Place.

Dhyāna – Meditation.

Draṣṭuḥ – The Seer, one who sees, observes and experiences.

Dṛg Dṛśya Viveka – *Dṛg* means 'Seer', *Dṛśya* means 'the seen', and *Viveka* means 'discrimination and understanding'.

Duḥkha – Pain, sorrow, misery, suffering.

Dveṣa – Aversion.

E

Ekāgra – One-pointed.

G

Guṇas – 'Strands' or 'ropes' that bind the soul to material existence. The three energy forces (*guṇas*) that materiality operate through are *sattva* (subtle matter of pure thought), *rajas* (energy) and *tamas* (inertia).

H

Hiraṇyagarbha – Cosmic Self. Also known as *Sutrātma* (thread-soul of the universe) because it binds all the constituents of the universe together.

Hong Sau – Kriya meditation mantra, that means 'I am He', affirming the nature of the Spirit within. It deepens the concentration and brings inner calmness.

I

Iḍā nāḍī – The left subtle energy channel in the subtle body.

Indriyas – Sense organs of cognition and action: *manas* (thinking or recording mind), the five *jñānendriyas* (organs of perception: ears, eyes, nose, tongue and skin), and the five *karmendriyas* (organs of action: vocal chords, hands, legs, genitals and anus).

Īśvara – God.

Īśvara-praṇidhāna – Constantly keeping the Divine Presence in the heart.

J

Jagrat – The wakeful state.

Janma – Birth.

Jarā – Old age.

Jñana – True spiritual knowledge, or wisdom to be known.

Jñānendriyas – Organs of knowledge: hearing, touching, seeing, tasting and smelling.

K

Kaivalya – Final liberation, absolute freedom.

Karmendriyas – The five organs of action: verbalisation, apprehension, locomotion, excretion and procreation.

Kleśas – Afflictions.

Kṣāntiḥ – Acceptance; forbearance; tolerance.

Kṣipta – Restless; disturbed.

Kuṇḍalinī Śakti – The dormant spiritual energy or psychic power lying coiled-up like a serpent at the base of the spine. *Śakti* is the kinetic aspect of the Ultimate Principle; the power that permeates all creation; *Śakti* is also the divine consort of *Śiva*.

M

Manas – Faculty of indeterminate knowledge; that part of the mind that receives impressions through the senses from the external world, but does not come to a final determination; deliberation.

Moha – An attachment.
Mokṣa – Liberation.
Mṛtyu – Death.
Mūḍha – Dull and preoccupied; stupefied.

N

Nāḍis – Subtle channels of energy in the astral body, of which there are 72,000.
Nidra – Sleep.
Niruddha – Restrained; controlled.
Nirvikalpa-samādhi – Superconscious state in which there is direct perception of the bliss of the soul or Self, and a total loss of any sense of duality.
Nityatva – Constancy; steadiness.

P

Para Brahman – Supreme Self.
Piṅgala nāḍī – The right subtle energy channel in the subtle body.
Prājñā – 'Knower', undivided consciousness. Associated with *Īśvara* (God), the source of all conscious souls.
Prakṛiti – Eternal principle of matter; primordial energy of creation.
Pramāda – Carelessness.
Prāṇa – Life force.
Pratyāhāra – The state in which the senses are withdrawn from the mind, and appear to be one with the mind.
Pratyaya – Objects.
Puruṣa – The pure, eternal and unchanging Consciousness; the Self, the eternal conscious principle.

R

Rāga – Attachment. *Rāga* comes from *raj* ('to be excited') and can mean desire, attraction or attachment.
Rajoguṇa – Quality of activity or passion.

S

Sādhanā – Spiritual practice.

Samādhi – *Sam*, 'with'; *adhi*, 'Lord'; 'union with the Lord'. Or *sam-ā-dh ā*, 'to hold together'. The state of superconscious absorption (*samādhi*) that is attained when the meditator, the process of meditation and the object of meditation (God) become one.

Samāhita citta – Steadiness of mind.

Saṁprajñāta samādhi – *Samādhi* (superconsciousness) with wisdom (*prājñā*) or perfect knowledge.

Saṁśaya – Doubt.

Saṁskāras – Deep active seed impressions in the subconscious mind.

Śankarācārya – (Sankaracharya) A great Sage born in the southern state of Kerala, India around 820AD. His name is synonymous with the revival of *Advaita Vedanta* philosophy in India. It is said that he mastered the Vedas by the age of eight, and at sixteen, wrote his commentary on the *Brahma Sūtras*.

Sat-Cit-Ānanda – Ever-existing, ever-conscious, ever-new Bliss, the spiritual nature of the inner Self.

Sattva guṇa – Quality of harmony. A person in whom *sattva* is predominant is contemplative and peaceful.

Śaucaṁ – Inner and outer purity.

Sevitva – To inhabit or resort to.

Siddhāsana – Adept's pose. *Siddha* means 'accomplished', perfected', and is also used to refer to a perfected yogi or sage who has attained the highest spiritual perfection or enlightenment, and who possesses great spiritual powers called *siddhis*. The best sitting posture for meditation.

Sthairyam – Steadfastness.

Styāna – Dullness.

Sukha – Pleasure.

Sushupti – Dreamless deep sleep state.

Suṣumnā nāḍī – Main subtle energy channel in the subtle body.

Svādhyāya – Self-study; introspection.
Svapna – The dream state.
Svarūpa – One's own real nature.
Svayam-prakāsha – Self-luminous. The Self requires no other light for its manifestation.

T

Taijasa – 'Luminous one'. The manifestation of the individual in the subtle body that develops a false identification of the self with ego.
Tamas – Darkness, inertia, stability.
Tanmātra – Five subtle elements: sound (*śabda*), touch (*sparśa*), colour/form (*rūpa*), taste (*rasa*) and smell (*gandha*).
Tapas – *Tapas* or *tapaḥ* literally means 'to heat up' or 'to burn'. *Tapas* is purifying, it burns the impurities and desires in the mind.
Turīya – The fourth state of consciousness, in which the consciousness merges into the *ātmān* (Self).

U

Uḍḍīyāna bandha – Abdominal lock that encourages the *prāṇic* energy to flow upwards through the *suṣumnā* channel in the astral spine.

V

Vairāgya – Derived from viraga. The prefix vi means: devoid of; free from; very special; unique. Raga means 'colouring', 'attachment'. *Vairāgya* refers to the state in which the mind is stable and is not coloured or affected by thoughts, speech or deeds. *Vairāgya* is detachment from karmic impressions and the actions propelled by them. *Vairāgya* is a state of awareness free from all attachment.
Vāsanās – 'Colouring'. Unmanifested tendencies that 'colour' the mind affecting your desires, feelings, thoughts and intentions. Latent tendencies.

Vidyā – Self-knowledge.

Vikṣipta – Distracted; distracted state of mind. (Third of the five states of *citta*.)

Virāt – Universal cosmic form. The fully manifested macrocosm encompassing all the aggregates of the perceptible and tangible phenomenal universe.

Viśva – The individual self, the experiencer of the waking state bound and conditioned by matter, and associated with the phenomenal world and the gross body.

Vivikta – Separate.

Vṛttis – From the verb root *vṛt* which means 'vortex'; whirlpool, to whirl, to revolve, movement. Subtle vortices of mental energy that revolve and spin in the mind.

Vyādhi – Disease or illness.

Bibliography

Kriyananda, Swami, *Revelations of Christ*, Nevada City, CA: Crystal Clarity Publishers, 2006

Mother Theresa, *Everything Starts from Prayer*, Ashland, Oregon: White Cloud Press, 1998

Scofield, CI, *Oxford NIV Scofield Study Bible*, New York: Oxford University Press, 1984

Sturgess, SR, *The Yoga Book*, London: Watkins Publishing, 2002

Sturgess, SR, *The Book of Chakras and Subtle Bodies*, London: Watkins Publishing, 2014

Sturgess, SR, *Yoga Meditation*, London: Watkins Publishing, 2014

Sturgess, SR, *The Supreme Art and Science of Raja and Kriya Yoga*, London: Singing Dragon (an imprint of Jessica Kingsley), 2015

Venkatesananda, Swami, *Vasiṣṭha's Yoga*, Albany, NY: State University of New York Press, 1993

Vivekananda, Swami (1863–1902), *Religion of Love*, published by Swami Bodhasarananda, Advaita Ashrama Mayavati, Champawat, Uttarakhand, Himalayas, 2012

Yogananda, Paramhansa, *Autobiography of a Yogi* (reprint of the 1946 first edition), Nevada City, CA: Crystal Clarity Publishers, 1994

Yogananda, Paramhansa, *How to Be Happy All the Time: The Wisdom of Yogananda, Volume 1*, Nevada City, CA: Crystal Clarity Publishers, 2006

Yogananda, Paramhansa, *How to Be a Success: The Wisdom of Yogananda, Volume 4*, Nevada City, CA: Crystal Clarity Publishers, 2008

Yogananda, Paramhansa, *How to Awaken Your True Potential: The Wisdom of Yogananda, Volume 7*, Nevada City, CA: Crystal Clarity Publishers, 2016

Zambito, Salvatore, *The Unadorned Thread of Yoga: The Yoga-Sutra of Patanjali in English*, Poulsbo, WA: The Yoga Sutras Institute Press, 1992

About the Author

Stephen Sturgess has been practising Yoga and meditation since 1969, when he was first introduced to it by Swami Pragyamurti, a direct disciple of Paramhansa Satyananda Saraswati of the Bihar School of Yoga in India.

During those 43 years Stephen has studied, practised, and experienced the different paths of Yoga and meditation – *hatha*, *raja*, *kriya*, *kundalini*, *tantra*, *jnana*, *karma* and *bhakti* – which increased his spiritual insights, experience and spiritual knowledge. While following these different paths he studied under well known Yoga masters. These include three of Swami Sivananda Saraswati's (of Rishikesh) foremost disciples: Swami Satyananda Saraswati, Swami Venkatesananda and Swami Vishnudevananda. These inspiring Yoga gurus were making regular visits to London in the 1970s.

Stephen was initiated by Swami Satyananda Saraswati in 1979 and given the spiritual name of *Shankara*. It was also in this year that he received the 'British Wheel of Yoga' teaching diploma and began teaching Yoga.

Stephen also met and studied Yoga and *prāṇāyāma* during the 1970s under the expertise of Yogamaharishi Dr Swami Gitananda of Pondicherry, India.

In 1982 Stephen met Swami Kriyananda (a direct disciple of Paramhansa Yogananda, author of *Autobiography of a Yogi*) in London. The night after meeting Swami Kriyananda, Paramhansa Yogananda appeared to Stephen in a superconscious dream, and told him that he was his guru, and that the Kriya Yoga path is the path he should follow. Then, in 1983, Swami Kriyananda personally initiated him into the ancient science of Kriya that Mahavatar Babaji taught to Lahiri Mahasaya, and that was passed down in succession to Paramhansa Yogananda.

For 26 years Stephen led the Ananda Kriya Meditation Group in London; then in 2011 Stephen was ordained as a Kriya Yoga Meditation Teacher (*Kriyacharya*) to teach and initiate others into Kriya meditation by Roy Eugene Davis (a direct disciple of Paramhansa Yogananda), who is the director of the Center for Spiritual Awareness (Georgia, USA).

In addition to his primary devotion to Yoga and meditation, and related subjects, Stephen has a BA(Hons) Ayurveda Degree from Thames Valley University (2004). He is also a graphic designer, artist, and a writer. He lives in London and continues to guide and inspire others on the spiritual path of Kriya Yoga Meditation.

Stephen is also the author of *The Yoga Book*, *The Book of Chakras and Subtle Bodies*, *Yoga Meditation* (published by Watkins Publishing, London), and *The Supreme Art and Science of Raja and Kriya Yoga* (Singing Dragon Publishers).

Stephen teaches Kriya Yoga Meditation in London, and initiates those who have spiritually prepared and are ready for commitment to practising Kriya meditation.

Stephen can be reached at:
website: www.yogananda-kriyayoga.org.uk
email: stephensturgess@hotmail.com

Kriya Yoga Meditation Resources

Kriya Yoga Meditation Teachers, organisations and centres following the teachings of Paramhansa Yogananda:

Stephen Sturgess (UK)

Stephen Sturgess, *Kriyacharya*, is a disciple of Paramhansa Yogananda and was taught and guided in Kriya Yoga by Swami Kriyananda for 30 years, from when he first received Kriya Initiation in 1983. He was ordained in 2011 as a Kriya teacher (*Kriyacharya*) by Roy Eugene Davis (a direct disciple of Paramhansa Yogananda) to teach and initiate sincere Truth seekers into Kriya Yoga meditation. Stephen teaches the preparation Kriya meditation techniques in London, and gives Kriya Initiation only to those who are sincerely interested in spiritual awakening and Yogananda's Kriya Yoga teachings, and have done the necessary spiritual training. Awakening to Self-knowing and Self-realisation is a gradual process and requires self-discipline and diligent practice with love, devotion, willingness, right and positive attitude, and perseverance.

email: stephensturgess@hotmail.com

website: www.yogananda-kriyayoga.org.uk

Roy Eugene Davis (USA)

Roy Eugene Davis is a direct disciple of Paramhansa Yogananda. He offers spiritual support and resources, seminars and Kriya meditation retreats based on the teachings of Paramhansa Yogananda. He also gives Kriya Initiation.

Center for Spiritual Awareness, PO Box 7, Lakemont, Georgia, USA 30552

Tel: (001) (706) 782-4723

email: info@csa-davis.org

website: www.csa-davis.org

Ananda Communities

Ananda spiritual communities have a selection of instructional DVDs and CDs that cover preparation techniques for practising Kriya Yoga, including Yogananda's 'Energization Exercises'. Both Ananda and the Self-Realization Fellowship sell the 'Arm-rests' ('*Aum* Boards') for practising the *Aum* Technique.

Ananda Sangha (USA)

Ananda Sangha is a worldwide organisation founded by Swami Kriyananda, a direct disciple of Paramhansa Yogananda, which offers spiritual support and resources based on the teachings of Paramhansa Yogananda. There are Ananda spiritual communities in Nevada City, Sacramento, Palo Alto and Los Angeles, California; Seattle, Washington; and Portland and Laurelwood, Oregon.

website: www.ananda.org; www.expandinglight.org

Ananda Assisi (Italy)

Ananda Assisi is a spiritual community and Kriya Yoga retreat.

Ananda Assisi, Via Montecchio, 61, 06025 Nocera Umbra (PG), Italy

website: www.ananda.it

Ananda India (India)

Ananda India has spiritual communities in Gurgaon near New Delhi and Pune in North India.

email: ananda@anandaindia.org

website: www.anandaindia.org

Self-Realization Fellowship (USA)

Paramhansa Yogananda founded the Self-Realization Fellowship (SRF) in America in 1920 to make the teachings of Kriya Yoga universally available. The Self-Realization Fellowship has its headquarters in Los Angeles, California. SRF has more than 500 temples and centres around the world and has members in 175 countries. In India and surrounding countries, Paramhansa Yogananda's work is known as Yogoda Satsanga Society of India (YSS, www.yssofindia.org), which he founded in 1917. The SRF Lessons, an in-depth home study course which provides Paramhansa Yogananda's step-by-step instructions in his Yoga methods, including the Kriya Yoga science of meditation and his 'How-to-live' teachings, are available from the Self-Realization Fellowship. The SRF have many books available for sale written by Paramhansa Yogananda, a selection of DVD and CD talks and devotional music.

Self-Realization Fellowship, International Headquarters, 3880 San Rafael Avenue, Los Angeles, CA 90065-3219, USA

Tel: (001) (323) 225-2471; (001) (818) 549-5151 (telephone orders).

website: www.yogananda-srf.org

London Centre of Self-Realization Fellowship (UK)

London Centre of Self-Realization, 82A Chiltern Street, London, W1U 5AQ

website: www.srf-london.org.uk

Acknowledgements

Many thanks to the meditator models who posed for the photos that I photographed for this book – Giulia Tripepi, Lina Kurlinkiene, Violaine Le Delezir, and Claire-Marie Longley. Thanks to the John Hunt Publishing team who made the publishing of this book possible.

BOOKS

O-BOOKS
SPIRITUALITY

O is a symbol of the world, of oneness and unity; this eye represents knowledge and insight. We publish titles on general spirituality and living a spiritual life. We aim to inform and help you on your own journey in this life. If you have enjoyed this book, why not tell other readers by posting a review on your preferred book site? Recent bestsellers from O-Books are:

Heart of Tantric Sex

Diana Richardson

Revealing Eastern secrets of deep love and intimacy to Western couples.

Paperback: 978-1-90381-637-0 ebook: 978-1-84694-637-0

Crystal Prescriptions

The A-Z guide to over 1,200 symptoms and their healing crystals

Judy Hall

The first in the popular series of four books, this handy little guide is packed as tight as a pill-bottle with crystal remedies for ailments.

Paperback: 978-1-90504-740-6 ebook: 978-1-84694-629-5

Take Me To Truth

Undoing the Ego

Nouk Sanchez, Tomas Vieira

The best-selling step-by-step book on shedding the Ego, using the

teachings of A Course In Miracles.
Paperback: 978-1-84694-050-7 ebook: 978-1-84694-654-7

The 7 Myths about Love...Actually!
The journey from your HEAD to the HEART of your SOUL
Mike George
Smashes all the myths about LOVE.
Paperback: 978-1-84694-288-4 ebook: 978-1-84694-682-0

The Holy Spirit's Interpretation of the New Testament
A course in Understanding and Acceptance
Regina Dawn Akers
Following on from the strength of *A Course in Miracles*, NTI teaches us how to experience the love and oneness of God.
Paperback: 978-1-84694-085-9 ebook: 978-1-78099-083-5

The Message of A Course In Miracles
A translation of the text in plain language
Elizabeth A. Cronkhite
A translation of *A Course in Miracles* into plain, everyday language for anyone seeking inner peace. The companion volume, *Practicing A Course In Miracles*, offers practical lessons and mentoring.
Paperback: 978-1-84694-319-5 ebook: 978-1-84694-642-4

Rising in Love
My Wild and Crazy Ride to Here and Now, with Amma, the Hugging Saint
Ram Das Batchelder
Rising in Love conveys an author's extraordinary journey of spiritual awakening with the Guru, Amma.
Paperback: 978-1-78279-687-9 ebook: 978-1-78279-686-2

Thinker's Guide to God
Peter Vardy
An introduction to key issues in the philosophy of religion.
Paperback: 978-1-90381-622-6

Your Simple Path
Find happiness in every step
Ian Tucker
A guide to helping us reconnect with what is really important in our lives.
Paperback: 978-1-78279-349-6 ebook: 978-1-78279-348-9